Please, let me go

Please, let me go

The horrific true story of a girlys life in the hands of sex traffickers

Caitlin Spencer
with Linda Watson-Brown

AMARYLLIS

First published in India by

An imprint of Manjul Publishing House Pvt. Ltd.
7/32, Ansari Road, Daryaganj, New Delhi 110 002
Website: www.manjulindia.com
Registered Office:
10, Nishat Colony, Bhopal 462 003 - India

First published in the UK in 2017 by John Blake Publishing Ltd.

ISBN 978-93-81506-63-9

This edition first published in 2018

Cover photograph: Aleksandr Morozov/Getty images

Design by www.envydesign.co.uk

Printed and bound in India by Thomson Press (India) Ltd.

For all the girls that have been through the same as me.
For all the girls who have been ignored.
For all the girls who have been silenced.
For all the girls who have never been believed.

And for the ones who are fighting for them.

I hope this helps.

Caitlin x

This book is a work of non-fiction based on the life, experiences and recollections of the author. The names of people, places, dates, sequences or the details of events have been changed to protect the privacy and identity of the author and her children.

Contents

Prologue

I have a problem with waiting in rooms.

Actually, I have a *lot* of problems with them. When I'm there alone, but I can hear other people; when I don't know who'll be coming in or what will be expected of me; when I'm waiting to find out what will happen to me for the next hour or afternoon or day. It's not surprising, really. Over the years I've waited in many of them more often than I could even begin to count, and I don't remember the outcome ever being a good one.

This time, today, I have more information than I did then but I'm still nervous. I can feel my stomach as it turns somersaults, I can hear my heart pounding, so I try to concentrate on what I *do* know.

I'm meeting a woman.

She only wants to talk to me.

There will be cameras, but I'm safe.

I'm here because I choose to be here.

My story will be heard.

When I waited in rooms before, they were sometimes in houses, sometimes in flats. Often I was in a hotel, sometimes a posh one, sometimes a budget one. I would be meeting men. 'Meeting' – that isn't quite right, is it? We weren't going to chat, we weren't lovers grabbing a few stolen moments.

Those men, those rooms…

They were buying me.

I have flashbacks all the time. It started when I was so young and, to be honest, I'm not even sure it's over. They have done so much damage to me – emotionally, physically, psychologically, that I think I'm probably broken beyond all repair. But I'll fight. Today is part of that fight. This woman wants to hear my story. She's going to talk to me, she's going to listen, then she's going to add my words to the words of other girls and women like me, and she says maybe someone else will listen too. I'm not so sure about that bit – I think most people want to close their eyes and ears to what happens on their streets, in flats and houses across the country, and in hotel rooms. They want to pretend that only certain types are involved in this 'sort of thing'. They'd rather it was one section of society, or one type of girl. They feel more comfortable putting labels on it and saying it would never happen to them, to anyone they know.

But those girls, those women, are someone's daughters.

Those men are someone's sons.

And fathers.

And husbands.

I want to speak out, I really do, but it's so hard to trust anyone because I've been through so much. I want to tell my story to help others and to prevent more young girls from a life of horror – but the flashbacks never stop, the nightmare is far from ending. Sitting here, waiting for my story to be heard, I just want to leave, I want to run. I could do that – I could walk out of that door right now… But the thing is, I always could. The hold they had on me wasn't one of locks and chains, the only key I needed to access was one within me. And that was hidden for so very long.

So, I'll do this. I'll speak out and maybe, just maybe, that'll loosen the chains no one can see and help me find some freedom from my own past. But it won't be an easy journey…

Are you ready to take it with me?

CHAPTER 1

before

I think of my life in blocks. There was before, then there was when it all started and what happened, and then there's now. Most of the time, I am stuck in the middle section – it's hard not to be. Not only did it take up most of my life, it's impacted on everything. I think it's even impacted on my 'before' because I can't have the memories of then without knowing what's coming.

As I've written this, I've found it hard to think of anything good. It's not that I don't have any nice memories, it's that sometimes I deny myself thinking of anything that's good because I know it will all become tainted when the other memories come rushing in. But I have to try, I know that. It's only if I show you just how ordinary a child I was that you'll see just how low I was taken, just how broken they made me.

Before it all began, in the first block, I was a very naïve girl – I didn't have a wild life and I wasn't always trying to be something or someone else. I was a skinny little thing, and I usually had scraped knees and a muddy face because I liked to be outside all of the time. I don't know if I was always like that but certainly, from the time I was about ten, I never wanted to be inside.

My life was quite straightforward when I was on my own. I had a younger brother called Sam, and I had a mum and dad. Sam was a lot younger and we were very different so I never hung around with him – in fact, I preferred to be as far away from him as possible. I was such a tomboy, with secret hiding places, who loved climbing trees and spending all day in the fresh air. I would grab an apple from a tree for lunch, climb over fences, paddle in streams, run everywhere. I just loved being outdoors – and I loved animals. Always on the lookout for strays, I was constantly drawn to anything that I could cuddle. From an early age I knew that I would want to work with animals when I grew up, but that seemed a long way away, and for the time being, I just wanted to have some of my own.

I was always bringing kittens home – our neighbour's cat seemed to be permanently having litters and I vividly recall one day when the neighbour said to me, very casually, 'If I don't find homes for these, I'll have to drown them.'

Drown them! I was horrified. I got very emotional about animals and the thought of someone willingly, knowingly, causing any harm to any living creature made me feel ill. I made a decision there and then, without thinking of the consequences: I'd save them. So I took two of the kittens home and hid them from my mum. I didn't really think it through, I just wanted to get them away from the awful woman. When I held them in my arms, I could have wept with how much love I felt. They were so tiny, so young that I could feel their little ribs beneath my fingers and the beat of their hearts when I held them. I loved the way they jumped up to rub their heads against my chin, and how they tried to nip me with their little teeth. I didn't really think ahead – I just loved them immediately and wanted to keep them.

I had a massive cupboard in my bedroom and managed to keep them there for two whole weeks. We had cats anyway, so I just pinched some of their food every day and took it up to the little ones. I spent hours playing with them, cuddling them, emptying their makeshift litter tray – but when Mum found out, she went mad. I don't know why; surely two more cats wouldn't have hurt? They were only little, but she wouldn't budge, so the kittens went. Mum found another home for them and I cried my heart out. I was always able to cry over animals, always able to relate to their pain, and I could never bear the thought of someone harming them.

We also had rabbits that were always having babies, we had pigeons that the person before us had left when they moved, and we had the cats. But it wasn't enough. I'd have filled the house with animals given half the chance. I think that's why I loved the outdoors too. Not only was there a lot of wildlife, but I always lived in hope that I'd find some abandoned or needy creature that I could save. I was drawn to them – drawn to helping them. With my friend, Lucy, I could spend all day outside. We'd go off into the countryside to some closed paintball woods as soon as we got changed from school, or at weekends and school holidays. I hung around with Lucy a lot while I was at primary school, and until I was about fourteen. In those days I was quite happy, at least for the bits that I can remember, but there are some gaps in my memory now – I've even lost the happy bits, bits I would love to remember.

Lucy was a straight-A student who never did a thing wrong. Her mum was very strict, but I think Lucy was just a good child rather than one who was kept in line by her parents. I got into trouble sometimes, like most kids, but I was actually a very innocent little girl. Even when I became a teenager, I had no interest in boys and very little knowledge of sex, apart from what I learned in school lessons. I'd never kissed anyone, never even held hands with a boy, and I didn't want to either. A perfect day for me was going out on my bike first thing in the morning, meeting up with Lucy, taking some carrots to the horses in a local field, and building a den or hiding in a haystack. The only time I really got in trouble was when I was protecting animals. I remember someone's mum turning up at our door once, complaining I'd punched her son.

'Is that true?' demanded my dad.

'Absolutely,' I told him. 'Why wouldn't I? He was kicking a cat.'

'Kicking a cat?' repeated Dad.

'Kicking a cat,' I muttered, walking off. 'Got what he deserved.'

I got in a row with Mum and Dad for that, but I couldn't really understand why; this boy had been attacking an innocent animal but I was the one getting into trouble for hitting him. It seemed mad to me and it certainly didn't make me stop. There was a boy I caught stabbing hedgehogs with a dart – how can people even *think* to do these things?

***

Mum, Dad, my little brother Sam and I lived in a three-storey terraced council house in Coventry and my room was at the very top. I spent all my pocket money on those magazines that told you all about cats and dogs – how to look after them, stories about them, everything to do with them – and I cut out all of the cute images to plaster everywhere I could; the walls were covered in animal pictures. I also loved anything to do with Disney. I held onto those childhood things for longer than might be considered 'cool' but that didn't bother me – I had no interest in being part of a cool gang anyway.

When I went to high school, I made a new friend. Lucy was still around, but she was much smarter than me so we didn't have any classes together. I loved being with her and we never fell out, not even once. But she was always destined to do well, so I was really happy when I met Danny. Looking back, it's a miracle I met him at all as he was hardly ever at school. He was from a family who were notorious in our area – they were violent and couldn't care less about rules. Danny learned that at an early age and only went to school when he felt like it. You just didn't mess with them and that's how he got away with bunking off – even the teachers wouldn't risk getting into an argument with that family.

Danny was so streetwise but an absolutely lovely boy in the middle of a family who would give you nightmares if you got on the wrong side of them. But there was nothing between us – we were just kids and I think he looked on me as a little sister.

I saw Danny every day, but I was usually the only one who had been to school. Every day, he met me with a baseball bat in his hand, although no one dared to mess with him anyway. This was the late nineties and the area was already becoming known for having men who targeted young girls and looking back, I now think that Danny probably saw a lot of what was going on. He was protective of me too and wanted to look out for me. I was once attacked by an older boy at school, who tried to feel me up when I was about twelve and that made Danny furious.

'I'll kick his fuckin' head in,' he swore to me. 'What the fuck does he think he's playing at, trying it on with you?'

I still saw Lucy when I could but I spent most of my spare time with Danny. He loved animals just as much as I did, and I think that's what really bonded us. We weren't exactly sensible, though. One day, he met me after school with a grin on his face.

'Guess what?' he said. 'You know that mad old woman who lives three streets down from you and looks like she's been dragged through a hedge backwards?'

'Mrs Johnson?' I said, already worried. 'Oh no, Danny! What have you done? She's got such a temper on her.'

'No, no,' he reassured me. 'She's selling hamsters! They're only £1 each – want to get a couple?'

'Yes! Yes, I do!' I replied immediately. 'But they don't do very much, do they? I mean, I'd love them anyway, but…'

'"Don't do very much"?' said Danny. 'They can do whatever we want, they can go wherever we go. Are you up for it, Caitlin?'

So, off we went. The toughest twelve-year-old in Coventry and me, nothing more on my mind than hamsters. We adored those little fluffy bundles, so much so that we used to take them out for day trips on our bicycles, riding round with them in the baskets. I guess it was funny, really – this tough lad whose family would chase you with an axe down the street if you looked at them the wrong way, but who'd raised such a kind, caring boy.

Looking back, I wish Danny had stayed in my life

and that I'd confided in him about everything. Maybe having someone like him or his family on my side would have helped me more than anyone else did. However, when I was fourteen, everything changed. Mum and Dad announced that the area we lived in was getting too rough – I've no idea if the fact that Danny was my best friend was part of that – and we were moving house. They'd applied for new jobs and wanted to get away from somewhere they thought just wasn't safe anymore, with its petty crime and air of general desperation.

So, with new jobs that would take them out of the house for long shifts at a time as they managed a local nursing home, they decided it was the perfect opportunity to get us all a new place in suburban Coventry. I was slightly worried about such a big change as I'd be moving school, away from my friend Lucy, and I wouldn't be able to see Danny. But I was also excited about all the little things, like a new bedroom and a different area to explore.

It was all straightforward for my brother Sam as he was given a place at the local junior school really quickly, but for me it was more complicated. There were no spaces available and I had to wait for an appeal with the local council to find in favour of me being accepted, or wait around to see if someone else left the area and made a space available in the local comp. It seemed to take forever and I spent a lot of time home alone. Mum and Dad were always at the old folks' home, trying to sort out the problems they had inherited, and I was really bored. Without Lucy or Danny, I didn't go out as much and there was a lot less to do in terms of wandering around the woods or the paintball site, as I was used to doing.

I was finding it hard to fill my days and there was no sign of the school situation changing in the near future, so I decided that I would find a job. Like many teenagers, I felt that I was more adult than I actually was and of course I knew best. Looking back, that was a ridiculous belief given how naïve and shy I had shown myself to be, but I guess all of that time alone in my room had made me think I was something I really was not. I would end up paying a terrible price for my misplaced confidence.

So I got a copy of the local *Friday Ads* paper, and started to circle a few jobs – shop assistant, general dogsbody in a hairdresser, that sort of thing. I really had to gather my courage to call any of them, but it was a waste of time. As I stuttered my way through the conversations, they all said pretty much the same thing.

Do you have any experience?

No.

Are you sixteen?

No.

What age are you then?

Fourteen.

What sort of work have you done then?

Well, nothing really.

Are you still at school?

Yes.

So, you're fourteen, still at school, and have no experience?

Yes.

Sorry, love. Come back in a couple of years.

But I didn't want a job in a couple of years, I wanted one now. Dejected, I went back to the paper for another look: there had to be something. I really couldn't see what I was qualified to do, but surely everyone had to start somewhere? I needed to stave off the boredom until my school placement came through and I wanted something to make me feel, well, normal – I was sick of being so dull.

There was really only one ad that didn't need someone with a track record in working a till or dealing with customers.

Models wanted.

I'd rejected that one on my first read, and my second, but I was desperate now. I didn't think for one second that I was model material, but maybe they could use my hands or something? The ad said that it was for a catalogue and gave a number to call. To this day, I don't know why I made that call or where I found the courage to do it, but I did. Sometimes you look back on your own story and you want to scream out, *Don't do it!* Looking back, I want to grab the phone from the hands of that fourteen-year-old and bring her to her senses.

Are you stupid? I want to ask her. *Catalogue modelling?*

Really? But I was naïve, and I did think this was a chance to change my life.

I suppose I got that bit – it changed forever as soon as I made that call. Was there a part of me that knew? Did I have any sense that reputable photographers didn't really put ads in the local free paper to get real models? No, I honestly had no idea – I was so innocent and I thought that was where most people found work. I didn't realise that 'most' people would also have run a mile, or they would have been switched-on enough to make the connections, to see it for what it really was. I just thought the same things I'd been thinking when I made every other call – *I hope they don't think I'm too young, I hope they don't need me to have had any experience.*

I have a horrible feeling in the pit of my stomach as I write this, because I know that all it would have taken to change my life would have been for one person to say, 'You can sweep up for a couple of quid on a Saturday, if you like?' That would have done it; that would have made me feel useful. I would have thought maybe there would be a chance, if I showed I was interested and was friendly enough, that they would take me on for more hours, and I would have a normal life.

Normal.

What I would do for that.

We can't change the past though, and we can't rewrite what happened.

Stop it! Go climb a tree, go find a dog to rescue, I want to scream.

But it's too late, too late.

The phone's ringing...

CHAPTER 2

glamour

'Gordon here,' the man on the other end of the line answered gruffly. 'Who's this?'

'Erm, well... my name's Caitlin and... erm... I saw your ad in the newspaper?' I said, hesitatingly.

'Did you now?' he said. 'What did the ad say, Caitlin? Do you remember?'

'Just that you wanted models,' I told him. I felt so stupid even saying the word – I was no model, and I was sure he knew that even without seeing me.

'And do you want to be a model, Caitlin?' he replied.

'Well... I think so.'

'You think so?'

'I want a job, a part-time job.'

'Just part-time?'

'Oh, yes,' I hurriedly told him. 'It would have to be part-time, because I'm still at school.'

'Well, you're not at school now, are you?' he pointed out.

'No, no, I'm not – I'm waiting to get accepted into my new school. That's why I need a job, but I would still keep the job when I go back to school. Maybe at weekends?' I wondered aloud, trying to think on my feet and desperately hoping he didn't think I was some silly little girl.

There was a bit of a pause, and I thought that perhaps Gordon was thinking I didn't sound serious enough about this – had I blown it?

'What age are you?' he asked me.

'Fourteen,' I whispered. I thought it best to tell the truth, because he would know as soon as he saw me, if it came to that, but I knew I sounded like a kid anyway.

'Fourteen,' he repeated. 'And you're not at school just now – so where are you?'

'At home,' I told him. 'Ringing round to try and get a job.'

'At home… on your own?' he queried.

I told him that I was and felt as if the job – which I hadn't thought I would ever get anyway – was slipping through my fingers. I sounded such an idiot, such a *child*.

'You know what, Caitlin? I might have a job that would be right for you – well, if you're the right sort of girl, that is. I provide models for very reputable catalogues you know, no rubbish, but we'd have to check and see whether you were what I need. There is a problem though.' My heart sank. 'There are an awful lot of girls keen to do this – I'd need to see you very soon. Do you think that's possible? Could we do that?'

It was like a lifeline. I was doing nothing, and it was only mid-morning, so I was free to meet him and might actually get a headstart on all those other girls.

'I could meet you today!'

'That sounds perfect,' he said. 'Listen, if you're at home anyway, why don't I just pop round?'

And that was it.

The deal was done.

I gave him my address and he was there within the hour.

I want to scream when I think of it, to turn back the clock, to ask that child, that me, what in the world was she thinking? He wasn't even that subtle. Catalogues. Checking I was home alone. Being much more interested when he knew my age. 'Popping round' almost immediately. He couldn't have been more obvious.

I didn't get ready as such while I waited, because there wasn't anything I could have done – I didn't own any make-up, and I lived in jeans and T-shirts, so there was nothing grown-up that I could change into. I spent the time on my nerves really – what would he think of me, would he laugh when he saw me, how had I even had the nerve to call him in the first place? I tried to imagine what it would be like if I did get some work. Wouldn't that be a kick in the teeth for my little brother who was always calling me horrible names! Wouldn't that show people I wasn't just some silly little teenager waiting to get into school again! I was torn – on one hand, I was wracked with nerves, on the other, I was already imagining how impressive my new job would be.

Before I knew it, the bell rang and I could see

Gordon's shadow through the frosted glass. My stomach was in bits, but when I opened the door and saw a clean, well-groomed man in his thirties standing there, I did feel a bit better. I had no idea – all that worried me was that he would think I was too childish, that I wasn't model material. I only wanted a part-time job to earn a little pocket money. The longer I was staying out of school, the less I wanted to go back – *maybe this could really work out*, I thought. *Maybe I could show I was a grown-up and make some money.*

I invited Gordon in and he sat on the sofa in our family living room, but there was something not quite right. He was obviously working himself up to tell me something, and I assumed he had decided that I was wrong for the job as soon as he saw me – I was too skinny, too young.

'The problem is, Caitlin,' he told me as I bit my lip and waited for inevitable excuses, 'the catalogue work I thought I had has fallen through. I got a call just before I got here. It'll come back, no doubt about it, but there is always such demand.'

I was disappointed but not that surprised. It had been a long shot.

'Well, thanks anyway,' I told him, starting to stand up. 'Sorry to have wasted your time.'

'Hold on a minute,' he interrupted. 'There are always ways round things. Do you know what would help? Do you know what would give you a chance?'

I shook my head. This was all new to me.

'Well, you'd be ahead of the game if you had already done a bit of modelling. Had a portfolio, so to speak and knew your way around it. Would you be up for that?'

'Absolutely!' I told him, not quite believing I might get a chance after all. 'What do I need to do?'

'It's glamour modelling that really makes you stand out,' he replied.

Glamour modelling? That sounded great to me. I was such a tomboy but the chance of being glamorous was one I wouldn't turn down at all, as long as he could help me with it. Maybe he would help me do my make-up, or introduce me to someone who could show me – perhaps he knew an older girl or maybe he had a partner who would teach me the mysteries of lipstick and eyeshadow as I was certainly clueless.

'You sure?' he checked.

'Definitely!' I said. 'Never been more sure.'

'Just one problem…'

'I know – but I can change that!' I blurted out.

'Change what?' he asked, looking confused.

'I can learn how to do make-up, I can learn how to be glamorous… I know I look like a silly little kid, but I can change, honestly I can!'

He stared at me.

'It's not that. It's not… make-up. You're too young, Caitlin – you need to be eighteen.'

My face fell. There was nothing I could do about that, was there? I'd thought a quick trip to the shops would do it, but I couldn't age four years overnight.

'There is a solution…' Gordon told me. 'If you're up for it, that is. It's difficult to tell these days with girls, but if you were willing to sign a form to say that you were eighteen… Well, who's to argue?'

'I'll do it!', I agreed instantly.

If all that was standing between me and this wonderful new version of Caitlin was a signature, I had no qualms whatsoever.

But I still didn't know what it was; I had no idea what

'glamour' modelling meant. I thought maybe he would make me look pretty in nice clothes – if he could make me look eighteen that would definitely help, wouldn't it? It would get the attention of my parents too and encourage people to see me in a different way and I wouldn't have to go to school either. In fact, if he could show me how to look that age, I could get one of the other jobs I wanted anyway. It was the perfect solution.

'Let's get started then,' said Gordon. 'Now, we won't be interrupted, will we?'

I told him that Sam was at school and my parents were out at work – we had the rest of the day ahead of us if we needed it. He must have thought all his Christmasses had come at once. I was gauche and innocent; I didn't even own a skirt, I was such a tomboy. The house was empty and I looked my age – I looked young. The last thing he actually wanted was for me to look 'legal'.

I never did get that form to sign.

***

I can see him in my mind's eye at the moment as if he

was sitting right in front of me. And I hate him – I hate Gordon more than anyone or anything else on this earth because it all began with him. I can see him sitting there, on our sofa, in our living room. He was wearing a striped shirt. He was quite handsome, I suppose, with pale skin and blond spiked hair. He smelt very clean and he was well-groomed, but there was also something about him that made me feel uncomfortable as soon as the talk turned to this so-called 'glamour modelling'.

'We'll take some normal ones on the sofa,' he began and, in retrospect I think it was the use of that word 'normal' that made me wonder for the first time. *If we started with 'normal', what came after that?* It was a fleeting thought; I'm not even sure it came fully to the surface, but perhaps that was him pushing the boundaries a bit, so that he could see how I would react. 'Close the curtains,' he told me. No 'please', no niceness, just a demand. It had actually changed very quickly.

I should have suspected something then. Closing the curtains made the light very dim and Gordon had no extra lights for his camera. He didn't adjust anything, or use any additional equipment, so I guess it was just a ruse. I never did see those photos. Maybe he never took any; how would I know? Perhaps he waited to start taking them later. He was extremely no-nonsense, snapping away at me in very ordinary positions, as if he was a bit disinterested by the whole business. But it didn't take him long to suggest that we move on.

'I think we need a different environment, Caitlin,' he said, packing his things into his holdall. He wasn't even waiting for my response, he had already decided. 'Have you got another room we can use? Actually, now I think about it, let's go to your room.'

My immediate reaction was, *Shit!* My room was so childish – it was full of Winnie the Pooh and animal posters. If I'd told him that he probably would have loved it, but I didn't. Instead I thought of something else – I took him into my mum's room as it was grown-up. Gordon didn't question it, he just settled down on the edge of the bed and took his camera out again.

'Come on then,' he said. 'Let's get started.'

It was gradual.

I can't imagine what happened will come as a surprise to anyone reading this and I feel such shame writing it but, slowly, he got me to take bits of my clothing off.

'Take your top off,' he said, as if it was the most natural thing in the world, but I was scared. I was shy and a complete stranger was telling me to take my top off – but I did it. I did everything he told me to because I was stuck in the house with a six-foot tall man who was making me feel uncomfortable, and now, just to make things worse, I was in my mum's room. This had been such a bad idea and it didn't feel very glamorous at all.

Just as I thought, *I can't imagine anyone looking at these pictures and thinking I'm a model*, it hit me: he had taken pictures of me. There were pictures of me. I know it sounds stupid, but as the camera was clicking away, I remember just telling myself, *Get it over with, then he'll leave.* But the thought that he would eventually leave wasn't such a comfort anymore – he would have photos of me with my top off.

Why didn't I just ask him to leave? Well, I was scared and he was big. His size scared me, his presence scared me, and he was very confident. At first I was standing up with my top off, then he told me to get onto the bed. I did everything I was told and then he pulled a pair of hold-up stockings from his bag and tossed them at me. I'd never seen things like that before – they weren't exactly what my mum wore.

'Put these on,' he snarled.

So I got up and went into the bathroom but I didn't know how to put them on. Eventually, I worked it out and with embarrassment washing over me, returned to Mum's bedroom. I felt stupid; I *looked* stupid.

Gordon didn't seem to think so. He nodded, took some more pictures and then said, 'Take everything off.' I still had my pants on, but surely he didn't mean for me to take those off? He did.

I was so scared, my stomach was churning and I cursed my own naivety. He never said what the photos were for at this point – so did I still believe it was for some sort of portfolio that would get me ahead of the game when catalogue work came in? I really don't know; I think I was on autopilot and it was the first time that I started dissociating too. Maybe it was survival instinct that made me do everything Gordon asked because I knew he could hurt me if he chose to. If that's what it was, I was an even bigger fool than I suspected.

But I didn't ask him anything; I was quiet and submissive, I did as I was told, almost thankful he wasn't touching me. However, after a while – I have no idea how long, I have no idea about any of the time frame that day, really – we both heard the front door open and then slam close. There were voices travelling upstairs as we heard footsteps head towards the kitchen – it was Sam home for lunch with some of his friends.

I jumped up from the bed and put my head round the door of Mum's room.

'Don't come upstairs, Sam, don't come up here!' I yelled. 'I've just got out of the bath!'

'Shut up!' my little brother yelled. 'As if I'd want to see you!'

I just need to keep Gordon quiet, I thought, *and then get rid of him once Sam leaves for school. This has been a terrible, terrible mistake, but he'll know now that he has to go. It'll all be over soon.*

I was more naïve than I had ever realised.

By the time I closed the door and turned round, Gordon was already taking his clothes off. He was behind me, standing at the end of the bed; he didn't stop removing them when I saw him.

I'd never seen a man naked before – I was in shock.

'You'll have to go!' I hissed. 'You have to leave right now!'

'You better be quiet or your brother will hear, and your mum will find out what you've done. Shut up and do as I say.'

If you're in that situation – you've invited a strange man into your family home and let him take naked pictures of you – how do you, as a fourteen-year-old, get out of that? There was no way, at least none that I could see. I know now that anything I would have faced would have been better – Mum shouting at me, Sam finding out, getting grounded for years, never being trusted again. Anything.

Anything.

He raped me. On the bed.

Gordon raped me.

He didn't use a condom – why would he? Obviously he knew that I would let him do anything he wanted. I'd never had sex before and he knew that, he could tell – I'd imagine it was very obvious. At one point, he actually laughed and said, 'You're a virgin, aren't you?' I didn't even answer that.

From that point on I dissociated very quickly – I didn't cry, but I knew it hurt. I cleaned up afterwards, terrified there would be evidence on Mum's duvet cover, never thinking for one second that it might be evidence I could use against him. All I can remember thinking was, *If my mum comes home, she'll kill me for being in her bed.* That was what concerned me more than anything. I thought I'd be in so much trouble: not him, *me.*

I heard Sam and his friends leave, and Gordon was quick to leave after that. I guess he'd got everything he came for – he had naked pictures of a fourteen-year-old and he'd raped a virgin. I can't help but think that was a good day's work for a bastard like him. And he had me wrapped around his little finger. I hadn't fought back at any point; in fact, I'd covered for him and made excuses when my little brother and his friends had turned up. That had been a potential escape route – what if they'd seen a man there? What if they'd seen me half-naked? Surely any of that was better than what had happened?

Before he left, Gordon made it clear to me that I was in a terrible place now.

'You wouldn't want your mum finding out what a bad girl you've been now, would you?' he sneered. 'That you called a stranger? That you invited me here? Let me in, brought me up to this room, took your clothes off, let me take pictures – *and* the rest. I wonder what she'd say? Just you remember, I've got lots of photos I could show her, show anyone really.'

'Please,' I begged him, 'please don't tell her.'

How stupid was that? He laughed at me, laughed right in my face – I guess he couldn't believe how well this had all worked out. There I was, pleading with him, the man who had just raped an underage girl, not to tell my mum things that didn't really matter. I should have been screaming from the rooftops, he should have been the one who was frightened about what I might do.

'Well, we'll just have to wait and see, won't we? Here...' he said, very casually, throwing £10 at me, 'buy yourself some better underwear for next time.'

The way he said it and the look on his face made it very clear to me that there was no questioning this: there *would* be a next time. He was in charge, he was calling the shots, and I had no say in the matter. Then he kissed me on the cheek and said he would be in touch. I saw him to the door and then I went upstairs, almost on autopilot and ran a bath. As the water poured, I slowly lay myself down on the floor. It was cold and I could feel the aching in my body, where he had pushed himself, and where he had violated me. The first time should never be like that, it should never be like that at any time for anyone. I was bleeding a bit, but I just felt so ashamed. So dirty and ashamed. As I lay there, the weeping began, and when I finally turned the taps off, my face was soaked with the tears I thought would never stop.

I got into the bath and then… nothing. My mind goes blank.

I must have got dressed again, because the next thing I recall is Mum coming home. I'm not sure how much time had passed – certainly a few hours because of the amount I can guess between Sam being there for lunch and the time it was when she came in – but I've no idea what else I did, it's just a void. When I try to think back, I remember those parts as if it was yesterday: I can see him in my mind, I can even smell him. I know that I was in agony and I remember the feeling of deep,

deep shame that washed over me, but there are gaps. I knew he had raped me because I knew what happened before and afterwards, and I recalled the pain (which I still had), but those memories were like snapshots, disjointed frames with blank scenes which no amount of effort could bring back.

I want to go back and save her – I want to save that girl, that child. And I want to do terrible things to Gordon, because that can't possibly have been the first time he did it – he was too confident, too well-rehearsed. I'm sure he ruined the lives of many other girls after me.

I want to save her – and I want to stop him.

The truth is though… we're only just beginning.

CHAPTER 3

next time

My childhood ended that day. In my darkest moments, I feel my life ended that day.

When Gordon left, there was no mention of the job or his story that I needed a portfolio. There was nothing other than his promise, his *threat*, that there would be a next time.

After that I had a lot of baths just like that one and I stayed in my room for days. My parents were too caught up with their work to notice. I sank into a deep depression and didn't see how things could change – I just knew that he would be back, but even if he disappeared for ever, he still had those photos.

When he did ring, I wasn't really surprised. Even as a shy fourteen-year-old, I knew he wouldn't let go of me now that he'd found me. I had this big, clunky Nokia phone that would look like a museum piece now, and when he rang, it was almost a foregone conclusion.

'Hello Caitlin,' he said, as if it was the most natural thing in the world. I'd grow to hate the sound of his voice opening conversations like that – and there would be plenty of them. 'Make sure you're ready – I'll be there in ten minutes.'

Ready for what?

He put the phone down before I could ask, but I knew I had to see him to pluck up the courage to plead with him to destroy the pictures. I hadn't gone to the police – I would never have had the courage for that – and I hadn't told anyone, just as he'd asked, so maybe he could do this for me?

As soon as he knocked on our door, I was terrified. I opened it to see the man who had raped and humiliated me, and I knew that I would never have the strength to say anything.

I was dressed in jeans and a loose jumper, but he threw some clothes at me.

'Put this on – we have someone we need to see.' A tight, short black skirt with slits all the way up the sides, it was hideous. I felt like such a fool wearing it, but I did. There was a tight top too, nothing like the baggy ones I preferred to wear.

'Get in the car,' he said, motioning towards the red Ford parked in our driveway. And so I did. I walked out from the safety – was it safe? – of my own house, and voluntarily got into the car of my rapist.

'Did you buy decent underwear, like I told you?' he asked.

I shook my head.

'Why the fuck not? I gave you the money for it.' The £10 he had thrown on the bed after he'd raped me. I hadn't gone out, never mind gone shopping – I would have been clueless about what to buy anyway.

'Well, you'll be wearing nothing then,' he said, obviously annoyed.

The skirt looked like it had thick gaps so you could see I had no knickers on. Gordon didn't ask me to put any make-up on and I know the reason now: he wanted me to look like a tart but he also wanted me to look my age.

He barely spoke to me on the drive, other than to tell me that we were going to Oxford to see a friend of his. I'd soon get used to his friends – that was often the way he described them. But this one, this 'friend' – this was my first. I didn't really say much to him either. I wasn't sure what was about to happen, but I knew it wouldn't be good.

***

It took us about an hour to get there.

It was an ordinary-looking residential street, with a row of ordinary-looking houses. I remember quite a few people walking about, and they all seemed to be Asian. I was pretty naïve and didn't really know how to recognise different ethnicities, but there was no one else white around, just me and Gordon.

He pulled up at a semi-detached house with a driveway, and parked there, just as he had at my house, got out of the car and said, 'Come on, get a move on,' as I just sat there, not really knowing what was expected of me. I expected it to be bad though – probably more pictures, otherwise why would he have got me to dress up in this horrible skirt? I had no idea who would be in the house, or the extent of what they might want, but I got out of the car. I had no idea what else to do – we were over an hour from home, and I was with someone who terrified me and who I already felt I couldn't refuse. So, yes, I got out – and, yes, in theory, it might be seen as voluntarily, but I was already feeling trapped.

I stood there, a bit behind him, as he knocked on the door. It opened almost immediately, as if someone had been standing behind it, expectantly. There was an old man standing there – well, he looked old to me, I'd guess he was in his sixties. Like everyone I had seen in the area since we arrived, he was Asian. He looked very normal, if that makes sense, with a beard and glasses. There was nothing out of the ordinary about him.

Gordon had a brief chat with him, but they were talking in quite low voices which made it hard for me to hear. It definitely seemed like they knew each other. The only thing that was obvious to me was that the old man passed him some money.

He didn't even try to hide it. It wasn't like some shady drug deal, he just handed it over.

'I'll wait outside,' Gordon told me, and shoved me over the doorway as he walked past on his way back to the car.

The door closed behind me, and there I stood, in my tarty skirt, with no knickers on, in front of a man easily old enough to be my grandfather and waited. In truth, I was waiting for him to bring his camera out. *I just need to get through this*, I thought. I knew Gordon would be furious if I made a scene, or just turned round and went back to his car, and I guess I also told myself that there were already pictures of me, so maybe this would be enough to get him off my back.

'This way,' said the man.

He went upstairs and I followed. The stairs ran straight from the front door and on the walls lining the way were family photos. A man – him, I guessed. A woman – his wife? They were surrounded by other people in some of the pictures, some children – was he a grandfather after all? It looked that way. This was definitely a family home, it just had those touches – I could even smell potpourri. That was a woman's touch, wasn't it? This definitely wasn't the house of a man living on his own.

He opened the door and revealed a room sparsely

furnished with a single bed and not much else – I think it must have been the spare room.

'Sit down,' he told me, gesturing towards the bed. So I did – I always did as I was told.

I waited for him to give me some more instructions, but he didn't – he just kept looking at me, staring at me.

Then he started touching me.

He lifted my skirt a little – not that there was much to lift – and shame flooded over me as I heard his breath get heavier. Then he undressed me and I felt so awkward. This man, this old man, with his wrinkles and his gnarled hands, touching me anywhere would have been horrific, but the fact that he was touching me in places that were so private made me feel sick.

I don't know how to put this, because I don't want anyone reading it to get any sort of pleasure from it or to think that I did either – I guess all I can say is that he was gentler than Gordon. I didn't like it at all, I hated it, but he wasn't deliberately rough with me. He didn't call me bad things. Gordon had been very rough indeed, Gordon had been horrible. This man was less aggressive; he was very quiet, as was the house.

He was a very quiet rapist.

I was worried about someone coming home as I'd seen the photos on the walls – where were these people? I remember him asking if I was OK before I left – and me thinking that was quite nice of him. *He wasn't nice though, was he?* My mind was already skewed about what made someone 'nice', I guess. He raped me – how could that be nice? He was an old man who had bought a schoolgirl. He had – somehow – passed his 'order' to Gordon and had me delivered to his house, while his family was out, to be used for his sexual gratification. That was not the mark of a 'nice' man.

He took me to the door, this kindly grandfather with his glasses and beard, as my legs shuddered in fright from what had just happened. I think I was in there for about ten minutes. He had known all along what he was going to do, and I can only assume he'd been preparing himself for it, looking forward to it.

Gordon didn't even get out of the car when I walked out of the door. I don't think he'd gone anywhere while I had been in there – there hadn't been enough time. He asked the man how he was – not how *I* was – then took me home.

After the old man, I didn't hear from Gordon for a few days again, but I think that was the breaking of me. I stayed in my room afterwards as I still hadn't been accepted into a new school. My parents said nothing about me being isolated, about me taking myself away from anything and everything. As a mum now, I look back and think, yes, they worked a lot, but how could they not see how I was? I don't blame them but I don't think I would ever be like that.

I can't remember what the next one looked like, I just remember him raping me. It was another house, I know that – another family home. Another Asian man. Of course I didn't want to do it, I never wanted to do it, but I do wonder why I let it get worse. I hate myself for that – I hate myself for not stopping it. And I hate Gordon more than anything. None of this would have happened without him; he was the catalyst and he was the one who kept it going. I found my voice after the third time though. I tried to stand up for myself and told Gordon, 'I don't want to do this anymore.'

'Fair enough,' he replied. 'It's up to you.'

'Really?'

'Absolutely. Completely your choice.'

'Oh Gordon, you have no idea…'

'I take it you'll be fine with me showing your mum your photo shoot though?'

'What?'

'If you don't want to help me anymore, I take it you're fine with me not keeping your photo shoot quiet? I'm sure your mum would be very interested to see what you get up to.'

'No, Gordon, please…' I begged.

'But Caitlin,' he told me, 'you are not a stupid girl.' I wasn't so sure about that. 'You can't expect me to just think this can all be swept under the carpet, you must know that I would do this – it isn't an empty threat. You decide to stop helping me, I decide to stop helping *you*.'

So how did it get to that? How did it get to a point where the fact that the man who had raped me and taken naked pictures of me at fourteen got to say that he was doing me a favour by not telling my mum? More to the point, why didn't I let him do that? Why didn't I just call his bluff? Surely, if he had done that, if he had shown Mum, that would have shown just what he had forced me into?

I have asked myself this so many times.

I have gone back over it so many times.

Why didn't I let him show Mum?

Why did I say, 'Fine, go ahead'?

Was it because, deep down, I thought she would blame me, not him?

Gordon used that threat for a while; it worked for a while too.

* * *

I went from little girl to working girl in a very short period of time. Gordon began calling on me regularly. He often punched and kicked me until I was submissive if I did make any noises about being uncomfortable or scared about meeting people. Most of the time he was careful to hurt me in places people wouldn't be able to see, but not always. I remember my ribs being bruised, making it very painful to breathe; I remember my nose hurting and not being sure if he had broken it. Other times, if he even sensed that I might object to something, he would remind me of the photos, and after not very long at all, he had even more leverage and started sharing me amongst other people, his 'friends'. And, by doing that, he controlled me still further.

Shamefully, I would also sometimes call him. On my old block of a mobile, or from a payphone, I would ring his number, hating myself for doing so. Why did I do it? It was bad enough when he called me, so why did I voluntarily put myself in his line of vision? I've asked myself that a lot – I think he had such control over me because of the photos, because of the rape, but also I think I was just a very weak person. I never really stood up for myself, and I never had in the past. I was so ashamed of myself that I wasn't really seeing Lucy or Danny around this time either, and I was so scared of my mum's reaction if she found out. Gordon sensed all of it, and a pattern of psychological abuse and dependency developed very quickly.

A shape developed to our contact with each other. There were never any papers, or the pretence of them, never any comments about my modelling career, or catalogues; never any more photographs taken by him actually. He got in touch with me through my mobile but he would also turn up at the house as he knew there was hardly ever anyone there. I was compliant because I was scared but I think that I was a very feeble person too – I just never said 'no'.

Usually, he would say there was 'someone' we needed to see when he turned up for me. It was me who needed to see them though – and there was no real pretence about what it would involve. I hadn't left my room in such a long time, apart from when I was seeing Gordon, but Mum didn't seem to notice anything; if she did, she certainly didn't say anything to me. I never went downstairs to use the computer anymore… I didn't have meals with them… I thought she would sense something and I'd get in trouble, but she didn't.

I was passed from men to men and Gordon kept using the threat of the photos and what I had done until I just couldn't see a way out. Soon I was seeing people more and more often.

Then, I think I'd just got so numb to what was happening, I started not giving a shit about the photos.

'I don't care, show her!' I snapped one day after we'd had the same circular conversation yet again. That was it – he started getting really violent towards me, obviously scared that his control was slipping. He only ever raped me at times like that too, and it was always in my own house, as if to show me that I was totally in his grasp. If I made him angry, he would say it was my fault. After I tried to assert myself, it just went from one guy to seeing more than one on the same day.

***

It took a while before I got accepted at school – so long that I had only six months to actually stay there before I could legally leave. I've no idea if my parents chased it up, or pushed for it – I wish they had, though. I wish I'd been locked up in a classroom from the day we moved house. I wish I'd stayed that little girl playing in the woods with Lucy. I wish I'd told Danny what was happening. I even wish I'd told him and one of his maniac older brothers had gone after Gordon with an axe and put an end to it all.

But that didn't happen, and I certainly didn't do anything to help myself. As far as Gordon was concerned, it was always, 'You have to see this person,' that was the phrase he used. And they were always Asian – I didn't know where from exactly – for me that had clicked quite early on. I was even seeing some of them more than once: repeat customers, I guess, for Gordon as I wasn't being paid for it.

I struggle with timelines so much, and sometimes things pop into my head that are the flashes of memory that I spoke about earlier. Around the time I didn't care about the photos anymore, there was one instance when Gordon went ballistic at me. We were at his house, where he did take me sometimes, and I remember the aftermath rather than the piece of time when he was forcing me to have sex. His house was vile. I can see the room we were in, a cheap, nasty place that was almost empty, with fitted, flimsy old-fashioned brown wardrobes along one wall. The walls were a creamy yellow and there was a thin, nasty brown threadbare carpet. There was no bed in there, he would just push me onto the floor, and I recall staring at the square, frosted window up above me, just trying to focus on something that wasn't him. I never knew anything about his personal life, but it wasn't the sort of place that had a woman's touch – God help any woman who would have been with him anyway.

I must have been blanking things out, but I came round after he had finished with me and I could feel the rough carpet under my body. I wasn't fully dressed and I remember clearly feeling that I'd had enough.

'I can't do this anymore!' I yelled. 'I can't keep having this happen!'

'Shut up,' he snarled, pulling up his trousers and getting ready to leave the room.

'I mean it, Gordon,' I continued, in a way that was totally out of character for me, 'I swear I've had enough.' He turned round, looked at me, and left.

I wondered if he was finally taking it in. Did he know that I meant it? I guessed he would just come back and tell me that he would show Mum the photos again, but I genuinely didn't care.

But, no, that wasn't what he did.

I heard a door slam, then the sound of his footsteps getting closer to the room. Then I heard the clank of metal. In his hand was a huge, thick chain, far too heavy for locking up a bicycle, so I'm not sure what it would have been used for. He was swinging it round, and he was grinning at me.

All I could think was, *Heavy. That is so heavy.*

That is going to hurt, Caitlin.

You've been a very silly girl.

There was no doubt in my mind that he was going to use it on me – he didn't make empty threats. Continuing to swing it, he bore down and landed the first blow on my back as I moved over to try and protect myself.

'Stop!' I cried out.

Whack!

Again on my back, then on my side, then my arm.

Then all over again – back, side, arm.

Back, side, arm.

I couldn't get away. The room was small and he was blocking the door, but where would I go anyway? I had no idea where his house actually was and needed him to drive me home again; I just needed him to get it out of his system.

And so he did. He exhausted himself with it.

'Now,' he said, panting, 'have you learned a fucking lesson, you stupid little bitch?'

I was too sore to even answer. He kicked me.

'YOU do not get to decide. YOU do not get to choose when this ends. YOU do what I tell you. Get it?'

I was choking on pain, gulping on the waves of

agony thudding through my body, but somehow I managed to nod.

'Get the fuck up then,' he said, 'so I can get rid of you.'

After that I was left struggling to walk and with some really nasty marks but there are no other memories around it. I must have crept back into my house, so no-one could see the damage he'd done.

These days I get really angry with myself that I have such spaces in my own mind, such gaps from my own life. I fill the gaps with self-loathing. In dark times, I can't help but tell myself that it was all my fault. I can even convince myself that it was my fault the day he raped me in my parents' house, on the stairs with his friend holding me down. He was so angry at me, and I can't even remember what led up to it. I remember trying to focus my attention on the side window of our hallway – I could see the light through it and so I let my focus go in and out, trying to lose myself in the sunlight as it streamed in and these men did awful things to me. I can't remember though what I did wrong to make him that angry. His raping of me that afternoon was really quick and it felt more violent than at other times, but that might have been because of the other guy holding my arm down on my side, and feeling really trapped in such a small space. Afterwards, I had a massive bruise on the inside of my upper arm where I was held and I remember not having to see anyone for a while after, probably a week or so at a guess.

My reward.

Over that first six months, it was scattered and unpredictable because Gordon had no pattern – I never knew when he would turn up. He didn't even ask if my brother would be home. Now I know that was part of the psychological control of it all: I could never settle, never rest. Always I would be wondering and waiting to see if, today, there would be another man. Even on days when I didn't see anyone, I had no peace. If I'd known in advance that a day would be free of it, then I could have relished it, but that, of course, would not have helped him.

He was very clever: he had found a stupid, naïve girl and he had turned her into pretty much a sex slave, working for him, earning for him, and doing it all in a way that meant no chains were required, no locks were needed. He didn't kidnap me, he didn't threaten to kill me. Yes, he was violent, yes, he was a sexual predator, but I went back to my own home every time. I was completely free to walk about if I wanted to, to go on with my own life, as long as I did what he wanted, when he wanted.

It was a perfect way of working for him. Even almost twenty years on, I still question just how much I was to blame rather than seeing it all as his fault. How good was he? How smart was he to be able to do that?

And how stupid was I? How incredibly, heartbreakingly stupid…

CHAPTER 4

stupid

The truth is, though, not every waking second can be horrendous. As time went on, it's certainly the case that the repercussions of my abuse had more and more of an effect on me, but back then, between the ages of fourteen and sixteen, I was going to school, which gave me some sense of normality. Gordon was often picking me up and taking me to his 'friends', but I did have that semi-structure to my life. The best thing, however, was that I had somehow found the strength to do something for me – and, by the time I was fifteen, I volunteered in a cattery whenever I could. It was usually on a Saturday that I found the time. For some reason, Saturdays were quieter – was it because Gordon's friends had family responsibilities then? Perhaps.

And I loved it there. I was just a general dogsbody (or catsbody!), and I adored any time I could steal cuddling the cats and kittens as they waited for new homes. I would have taken them all home with me if I could. It was my escape and actually quite a happy place to work as I would often see lovely families head off with their new pets and be delighted that they had found lovely homes. A glimpse of my old life.

Unfortunately, Gordon wasn't keen on me doing anything else and he made it very clear that I had no real freedom, that he was always watching me. I used to bike there and he would later say that he had seen me go past at a certain time, even though I hadn't spotted him at all. He would tell me details so I knew he was watching me but I never saw him, I just felt his invisible control; he knew where I was a lot of the time. I started to think he knew where I was *all* of the time.

He ended up being my reason for leaving too. My boss at the time actually saw a lot of the bruises I had from Gordon and started asking too many questions, checking to see if I needed any help, prodding around to try and work out why I was covered in them. I tried to always cover myself, wearing long-sleeved tops and jumpers, even when the sweat was pouring off me from the hard graft of cleaning out the cages, but that drew her attention too. Soon afterwards I began missing a lot of shifts as I would stop going in if I had any obvious marks on me. I find it odd now to think a total stranger could pick up on it so quickly and yet my parents turned a blind eye. Why did they not notice? I struggle with this a lot, to this day.

In the end, it was easier to leave the cattery – I didn't want to tell my boss anything as I was too ashamed, and I worried that Gordon would be violent towards her too. By then he was hitting me a lot, whenever he felt that the photo excuse didn't have the same power. When I was reluctant, he just shouted; he'd say that he was in charge, that it wasn't up to me to decide what I would do.

'I'll burn your whole fuckin' house down with your family in it if you don't do what you're told,' he would say to me.

'No, Gordon, no – please don't do anything to them,' I'd plead with him.

'OK,' he'd say. 'You can have a fire, you can have my mates come round to kick their heads in, or you can do as you're fuckin' told.'

I did as I was fuckin' told.

I wish I'd told Danny, I really do – he couldn't have been there all the time, but who knows? Gordon didn't know of him because he lived in Oxford, not Coventry, and I kept him secret. My own good memory, my own friend – although just in my head now. I was so isolated, and the mental control was complete.

By this stage, I was often having to see more of Gordon's 'friends' for quite a few days of the week. He had an awful lot of friends, it seemed – an awful lot of Asian friends who all wanted to have sex with an underage girl. I was physically sore all of the time and I think my body was often in shock. I'm not sure whether I thought, at that time, that it would end soon – maybe he would get bored, maybe 'something' would happen – but, if I did, it wasn't to last. I would soon feel that I would never get out of this.

After a while, the number of private houses seemed to

decrease and the location of the abuse changed. Often I was taken to buildings – flats and apartments – that were being renovated or rebuilt, so I can only assume that many of these men were landlords or in the property business in some way. It was also becoming increasingly obvious that taxi cab drivers were generally involved as they would be the ones often sent to pick me up, or be the ones abusing me. It was as if there was a network of these men, all of them wanting the same thing, an underage white girl to rape, and all seemingly completely unconcerned about whether there would be any repercussions if they did exactly what they wanted.

There was no air of secrecy to this – they operated as openly in daylight as they did in the dark. They would collect me during school hours if they saw me, or stop when I was walking down the street; they would turn up at my door or phone me – and I was so psychologically and emotionally battered that I went with them. I didn't shout and scream, I just accepted that I was the filthy white bitch they all called me. They had made me into that girl and I hated what I'd become so much, that I didn't think I deserved any better.

***

After about two months, I had started to see more than one man every day Gordon collected me and we always seemed to go to these flats or houses that were being developed, or renovated. Gordon would just drop me at the door and I would be taken in, then he would pick me up afterwards and drive me home. I rarely spoke to him then; I'd just sit there, in pain, often bleeding, often out of it from alcohol or drugs, desperate for my own bed in a house that didn't really feel like a home anymore.

By now it seemed as if I was always physically sore, as if every part of me was in pain. Looking back, I had been so violated at such a young age that there was bound to be a bodily impact. These were grown men who were forcing themselves on a skinny fourteen-year-old, who was certainly neither willing nor consensual, and my body paid the price for that (and still does to this day). Always I was in pain, not just between my legs but every part of me. How I ached. I lived in fear, not just from knowing that they could phone or turn up for me or pick me up off the street whenever they wanted to, but from knowing that I wasn't strong enough to say 'no', and feeling there was no way out. I was being sick all the time, almost as if I had permanent flu, and it was starting to annoy Gordon.

'You're quite the fuckin' princess, aren't you?' he'd snarl at me. 'Time to toughen up, stop trying to get attention.'

Of course the last thing I wanted was attention: I wanted everyone to ignore me, I wanted to slink away so that they would never see me again, but I never felt right, and it was increasingly hard to hide the physical side of that.

'Oh, for FUCK'S SAKE!' shouted Gordon one day, when I vomited just before I got in the car. 'Are you always fuckin' ill?'

I felt as if I was.

He stared at me as I cleaned myself up before getting in the car, but he didn't start the engine, he just continued to look at me.

'When were you last on?' he asked.

'On what?' I replied, not knowing what he was talking about.

'You know... *on*.'

I shook my head.

'What?'

'When did you last have a period?' he pressed me.

I had no idea.

'I don't know – I don't really get them, they aren't regular,' I told him, embarrassed that he would be asking this.

'Think about it. When?'

I had never really been that regular, but since this had all began, I barely bled at all. Well, not from menstruating – I had bled plenty from what they had done to me, but that was different.

'I don't know, Gordon – it's not like it should be. I don't come on every month, I never have.'

'So, you've got no period and you can't stop throwing up? Oh, FOR FUCK'S SAKE!' he shouted again. 'You're pregnant, aren't you? You stupid bitch!'

'No, no!' I insisted. 'I'm just ill – honestly, I just have a bug.'

But I didn't really think I had a bug – I thought my body had just gone into shock because of what I was being forced to do. I didn't know if I was suffering from any sexually transmitted infections because I was never checked, but most of the men didn't use protection when they were with me, so it was always in the back of my mind as a possibility. I hadn't really considered pregnancy though. I was only fifteen by this stage and it was a horror that I had pushed from my mind.

Gordon stopped off at the local chemist and got out of the car, coming back with a pregnancy test in a paper bag. He drove me home, knowing that my parents would be at work and my little brother would be at school, and shoved me through the door.

'Get in there and piss on the stick,' he told me, pushing me into the loo. 'I'll wait here – you show it to me as soon as you're done.'

So I did as I was told.

I always did.

I do wonder about that – why was I so easy to control? I'm not sure I'll ever know, but I do know that, then, I didn't even wait to see what the stick showed. I took it out to Gordon as soon as I was done and he stared at it blankly.

Within seconds, he'd thrown it back at me.

'Fuckin' idiot,' he said.

I looked at it.

Two lines.

Positive.

Pregnant.

Me.

He stormed out and I was left there, in shock, and wondering how in the world I'd explain this to my mum. That was all I could think: Mum. She'd be furious. I went to my room, curled myself up on the bed and I didn't cry, I know that – I never really cried very often. I felt numb again. It was as if there was always something else, something else to come along and make everything worse. But a baby… How could I cope? What would I do? Would they leave me alone if I had a baby? Would they take my baby?

For a week, I was indeed left alone – apart from phone calls. Gordon rang and he texted, told me to stay put and shut up. I tried to go to school a couple of times, but my concentration was even worse than usual.

About a week after the test, I got an abrupt text one morning, as soon as everyone had left for the day.

'Outside,' it said.

So I pulled on a thin jumper and slipped my bare feet

into some trainers. I hadn't been out of my room for three days, and had barely eaten, so I remember feeling quite weak. As I walked downstairs to the car, I was thinking, *Is it starting again?* Was he taking me back to those men, or was there any chance that now I was pregnant, he was coming to tell me that I didn't have to do it anymore.

The car engine was still running when I got in – he never really hung about.

'We're getting this sorted,' he announced as soon as we drove off.

'Getting *what* sorted?' I asked.

'That,' he replied, poking my belly as he drove. 'We're getting rid of that.'

I don't suppose I'd really thought of an abortion by that point as I wouldn't have known how to go about it; I should have known that Gordon would deal with it all. I was his property after all, and this was stopping me from working. I was still being so sick – in fact, I'd been sick just before I got in the car – but I hadn't thought this through. I'd only been thinking about whether having a baby would stop the men from attacking me, or whether they would take the child. I hadn't thought that there wouldn't actually be a baby.

We drove for about ninety minutes. Gordon barely spoke to me at all, apart from telling me how stupid I was. It was ridiculous – I had no power in this at all, so he clearly was only getting at me, as there was no way I could have forced those men to all use protection. If I'd had that sort of control over the situation, I wouldn't have been in it in the first place.

'I'm dealing with this, right?' he said, as he parked in a residential street in a London suburb.

I knew what he meant and I nodded. *I couldn't really have a kid, could I?* This was the right thing to do – but I was scared. I was *really* scared. No one knew I was here, no one but him knew I was pregnant. Anything could happen.

I remember thinking the house looked nice. Although small, it looked normal enough, as if a family could live there. Gordon took control of everything and I certainly got the impression that this wasn't the first time he'd been here. They barely spoke to me – no one asked how far I was gone, there was no counselling, no scan… I didn't even get my blood taken.

I don't even know if it was legal.

Somehow I doubt it.

I heard someone ask if Gordon was my guardian and he replied that he was – I think they may have spoken louder at that point so that I could hear what they said as I didn't hear much else. I was under sixteen, so I suppose they had to go through that ritual, but given it all seemed so dodgy, I don't know why they kept up that pretence.

A nurse – a *nice* nurse actually – came over to me while he was at the desk filling in some paperwork, and tried to talk to me. I know I'd zoned out, but she did manage to get my attention and I followed her through to another room. I hold onto the fact that I think she was nice because I was so desperate for someone to just show me some warmth that day, but she didn't even ask my name, so maybe it's back to me not really being a very good judge of character. Just as I thought men who didn't rip me wide open when they raped me were nicer than others, I thought a nurse who led me to a general anaesthetic in a backstreet abortionist without even asking my name was 'nice'.

I woke up feeling awful and then there's a gap again – I know that Gordon must have taken me out to the car but I think I was going in and out of consciousness. I'd had no real attention in terms of post-op care and I felt so woozy. It was terrifying, they couldn't have had any idea if I would have a reaction to the anaesthetic, but I don't think that mattered. I was in pain, groggy, and I sat in the front of the car thinking I'd never felt so ill in my life. Gordon said very little, but he was calm, he took it all in his stride really – I got the sense he had done it before, but I'm not sure if I thought that at the time or that has come as I reflect on it all.

I didn't want the baby, not really, but maybe it would have brought things to a head if my parents had found out. By then I was scared of everything – being pregnant, having an abortion, but my biggest fear was the fear of them finding out. I was more worried about getting into trouble with my mum than anything else, that was always what terrified me. The photos, the sex, being pregnant, having an abortion… Gordon had more and more ammunition, and I felt more and more alone. I was just a kid and I was in the middle of this worsening nightmare without a single person I could turn to.

He left me alone for a while though – almost a

month; he never checked up on me once during that time. I felt ill and tired for a while but I was so relieved to be left alone. There were no medical consultations or follow-ups, no blood tests to see if I was anaemic or anything. I was blanking things out by this stage, but not as much as I would as the years went on. I'd also started self-harming, although I would be lying if I said I could remember the first time I did it. It quickly just became something I did to relieve the emotional pain, to be able to feel something that I was in control of.

I would cut myself with razor blades that I bought, breaking them open and releasing the blade to cut my legs, chest, and stomach. Once I did my face and Mum did actually notice that but I said that a cat scratched me at the cattery (they thought I was still heading there every Saturday, like a normal girl).

At first I did it so that I was more unattractive but then it started to make me feel better. Soon I learned how to do it in stages – I started with small scratches then I held it in a certain way so I knew how deep it would go in, I avoided veins, I never went up and down, just across as I researched online how to do it the best way, the safest way. It was pain to focus on, not an attempt to kill myself.

I also made myself throw up a lot. I hate to label it as I stopped doing it easily enough so maybe it wasn't bulimia, maybe it was just another way for me to decide what to do in my own time, on my own terms. I would buy huge piles of sweets then make myself sick. That was very cathartic – I got a sense of controlling my own body. I chose to do it, no one was forcing me.

A small victory, but for a broken girl, it was all I had.

CHAPTER 5

one girl

My body was still recovering but it wasn't long before Gordon came back. My self-harming didn't seem to bother him either. I think there was some part of me hoping he would see that I was so dead inside that it didn't matter to me what I looked like to the rest of the world, but he couldn't have cared less. And the men he sold me to? It didn't seem to bother them in the slightest.

Day by day, week by week, month by month, the next two years of my life almost blend into each other. I've seen some of my medical records, which show that I was attending STD clinics and where it was noted that

I was suffering from 'depression', but nothing was ever done, no one ever joined the dots. I think my family just saw it as me being a typical grumpy and frustrated teenager...

For two long years Gordon was in control of me and during that time, I was always waiting, just waiting, never knowing when I would be called on. I had no idea who had fathered my baby – it could have been any one of so many. They rarely used protection – even after everything I'd been through – and clearly didn't care whether they were giving me infections. I assumed they didn't care about their wives either. I knew they treated them with absolute disdain as well because I'd heard them talking about them in horrible ways. I wonder now whether they chose to speak in English just to make me know what sort of men they were. They spoke to each other in their own language a lot, but there were occasions when I was there when they would change over to English and I can only think they had a reason for that.

I hated everything about them. There always seemed to be food either being cooked or being brought with them to the flats where I was taken, and the smell of it made me feel sick. Not that I was ever offered any, anyway. To this day, the jangling and clanking of South Asian music puts the fear of God into me as it takes me back. The mixture of sweat and lack of washing and the food smells that oozed from them – all of it recreates that time for me. I know people might accuse me of being racist because it makes it seem as if I hated them for being of that race, of that culture, but the truth is, that is how they were and how it was for me: it's keeping silent, it's ignoring these things that has allowed this sort of abuse to continue. As soon as anyone says things like that they are labelled and their experiences minimised or ignored because somehow we think racism is worse than anything – even the rape of girls, even the hatred of women.

Once I started back at school I was sent to an occupational therapist so someone, somewhere, must have noticed something too, but it never helped, it never went anywhere and I stopped going soon after. I didn't really talk to anyone at my new school – I was shy, I knew no one, and I was only there for six months anyway. Of those six months, I was taken out so often by Gordon I was rarely there. In fact, I was put in the naughty class because of my attendance. I was there with five other kids with behavioural problems to do only Maths, Science and English – the basics. It seemed they'd decided I was a naughty kid so I just needed to do the minimum, bide my time until I could leave and then we could all breathe a sigh of relief. No questions asked – as always.

Gordon would regularly pick me up from school – no one seemed to wonder who he was – and I missed so much that there was no chance I would ever do well academically. I'd have to walk out of lessons when he texted me to come, and he'd be waiting outside in his car. The teachers just thought I was being disruptive – they never questioned why I would do that when surely I should have been staying in school. Surely it would only be because there was someone I was more scared of? But that didn't seem to register with them.

I'd still be wearing my school uniform when Gordon would take me to men – it's sickening when I think of it now. How they must have loved that. Once I was out of school for the day, or he'd picked me up from my parents', that was it, I wouldn't get back until I was 'done' – and 'done' was starting to mean more and more men. The pregnancy and abortion hadn't changed anything – I was still a girl, just one girl, to be used by so many of them.

I left school at Easter, and I only had to go back for my GCSE exams that I did very badly in. By now I was dissociating so much, and I know my memories are fragmented, but I also wonder how these men managed. *How did they actually manage not to think about what they were doing?* Did they get off on the fact that they must have known I would never have chosen this, or did they just never think about it? Fathers, husbands, brothers, grandfathers... they had women and girls in their lives and although I knew, from what I heard, that they often disrespected those women and girls too, in public, they did pretend that they were good men. Perhaps they also had a feeling of protection from knowing that no one wanted to say the unspeakable – I knew by now that they were Muslim men, Pakistani men, and they were raping me because to them I was nothing more than 'white trash'.

Gordon would always wait for me and drop me home when I was done. There was no way my parents were unaware of this, but they were deliberately turning a blind eye to the fact that an older man, a *much* older man, was giving me an awful lot of lifts and calling for me on a very regular basis. More regularly now, he would take me to his house in Oxford, where he seemed to live with two other men. I've done a good job of blocking them out but I know they never touched me and I never spoke to them, but they seemed to always have girls round them – girls like me, young, underage, lost. Often I saw these other girls in rooms with different men and it was at that point that I first started to get the feeling that Gordon and his housemates were like our employers. It's not like I got any money from him – just £10 here and there – but I saw men pay him when he took me to the flats, and I knew there must be a system where he was renting out my body. It was a bigger system than I thought at first; it took time but once I started to piece it all together with these other girls, I realised there must be an awfully big market for underage girls as products.

Maybe that house was more of a working area rather than a home as it didn't look particularly lived in. I would see the others as Gordon took me past to another room, where I would be kept all day. Taken, in my school uniform, at fifteen years of age, to wait for a series of men who all blended into one. At that stage they weren't that nasty, they didn't always call me horrible names; they were just there for the one thing. I didn't think of it as rape really as I wasn't saying no, was I? Gordon always said I had to be 'nice' to them, that's all – I'd soon learned 'nice' meant shutting up and opening my legs.

I would look back on that time as not so bad really, given what was to come.

***

For two whole years Gordon was in control of me. I was completely broken, this little girl who was now a working girl, this child who was being used as a woman. By the time I left school for good, just before I turned sixteen, one thing had changed: Gordon wasn't the only one who was picking me up. Sometimes Pakistani men would come and knock at my door – by now I knew where they were from. They'd ask for me, and my parents would just call me down as if it was the most natural thing in the world. These would be

Muslim men in their forties and my parents never told them where to go, they never once said, 'Fuck off and leave our little girl alone.'

I want to go back in time.

I want to say, *why not?*

Why was I not worth protecting?

And I want my mum to save me. It's only natural, isn't it? It feels like the natural way of things – maybe you want your dad to beat the living shit out of someone, but you want your mum to sweep you up in her arms, hold you tight, and say everything will be OK.

Fat chance.

Mine just opened the door and told me someone was waiting for me.

I've asked her, of course I have, but she tells me that they just thought it was a taxi. So we leave it there – it's too big to unpack, it would cause too much pain, and I do feel that I have to protect her now, to not have her feel that she was responsible for any of this. But I do wonder, there would be two or three of them at the door sometimes, grown men asking for a young girl to come out – really? A taxi?

Ask some questions, Mum, I say, when I fall back into

time. *Please – ask anything, something, just don't accept it all. Save me.*

Although I was still so young, I had left school and had no plans for the future. There'd been no careers advice at school, and my teachers were just happy to get rid of me. God knows what my parents must have thought, but our relationship had really broken down by now. I didn't have anything else to go on to, which meant my life was all up to Gordon now; he was always in control. I still saw Lucy, though very rarely as it was hard for me to go and see her, and I know she suspected something was wrong. She could see that I was self-harming as some of my scars were obviously visible, and I had gone completely into myself.

I remember one day, sitting on a wall with her, knowing things were different between us and wishing it could all go back to how it had been. We had little to say to each other any longer, but as Lucy went to go home, I whispered, 'I have a diary.'

She looked at me and nodded.

Within days, Mum had 'found' it.

I think I knew what I was doing – I think I told Lucy so that she would tell Mum, and, though I couldn't say it to her face, I think I wanted Mum to take action. Even with the gaps in my memory though, I know she didn't do anything for a while.

'I've read your diary,' she told me in an offhand way and I held my breath, waiting for her to go on, waiting for her to do something, but there was nothing. I hadn't written down all that had happened – nowhere near – but there were lots of details about Gordon and what he had done. A day or so after she had found it, though, she came home early from work one day and there, sat on the chair in our living room, was the guy who Gordon had sent to collect me that day. He had on a red shirt, with a big gold chain – he was a massive guy and there was no reasonable explanation as to why he was there.

'What's going on here?' she asked.

He couldn't even be bothered making up a good lie. Instead he gave her some cock and bull story about taking me to London to do backing singer work. Of course she knew straight away this was complete nonsense as I'm tone-deaf, I can't sing at all. He then stood up and tried to get me to leave with him but she wouldn't let it happen and he had no choice but to leave. She took my phone from me and a few minutes later, Gordon rang.

Mum answered.

'You fucking pervert!' she screamed. 'That's it, I've had enough – I'm calling the police.'

This is something that stays with me – she said she'd had enough, so she did know something was going on, and she did stick to her word and called the police, just as I'd always hoped she would do.

But it didn't matter.

It made no difference at all.

'Oh yeah, we know of him,' said the officer who turned up. 'We know all about him – she won't be the first and she won't be the last. Him and his dirty pictures.'

It was so much more than that.

'What are you going to do?' asked Mum.

'Nothing we can do,' the officer said, pacing up and down, obviously annoyed. 'None of them will testify against him. Waste of time.' He sounded annoyed that this was happening. 'She wants to complain? She better be prepared then – she'll be on her own, she won't get any support. Better let her get it out of her system, she'll stop in her own good time.'

'Oh, get out!' said Mum. 'You're no bloody use! She won't be testifying and so you may as well leave.'

And he did – he left without a backward glance as if it had just been an annoyance to him.

Mum isn't tactile, never has been. She didn't comfort me, there was nothing along the lines of her saying she would sort all of this. People were deciding for me, it seemed. When the officer had said that Gordon was known, to me it was shocking news but I did know there were other girls – I had seen them, they were older, but it was obvious. I just prayed one of them would have the courage to do something – and do it soon.

When the police officer left, I just went to my room – there was no conversation. All my mum said was, 'Don't tell your dad.' How I wish I had; I wish I'd told Dad. I also wish I'd taken it further – I now think it was really odd that one police officer came on his own and dissuaded me like that.

Was Gordon being protected? I certainly wasn't.

***

Our relationship didn't get any better after that and I

think that my leaving school made Mum think I was a grown-up and needed to fend for myself because pretty soon after I sat my exams she kicked me out. That's a confusing memory for me too – if she thought these men who turned up were just taxi drivers, why was she so enraged that she wanted me out? If she thought I just needed to get whatever it was 'out of my system', couldn't I have done it under the safety of her roof?

By this time, I saw Gordon less and less. It had gradually turned into a situation whereby it was Pakistani men who were collecting me, taking me to their flats, and abusing me. He was hardly ever there – and then, one day, I realised I hadn't seen him for weeks.

My hatred for Gordon burned strong. I detested him with every bone in my body and it slowly dawned on me that he would never have let me escape his clutches unless there was something in it for him. When he disappeared and the others took over, I realised I'd been traded, like a piece of meat, between one controlling abuser and another – it was the first time I'd been trafficked.

Although men had been buying me for almost two years by this stage, it was through Gordon – now, I had different owners. I found a place to stay at a local hostel, helped out by my parents, and once I'd moved in I didn't hear from Gordon anymore.

These new men treated me very differently. At one time it would have been hard for me to believe it was possible, but they were worse than Gordon. It was never one at a time, there was never a day when they came for me and I would only see one man – I lost count.

I never thought it would get worse, but it did. They would come to the hostel, or see me on the street, drive me to a flat or a house, or to a particular chain of hotels. I hate them – they took me to those a lot, it was always that particular chain. I remember the colours so clearly. Even now, I can't bear to go in them and the TV adverts turn my stomach.

There was always one man walking in front of me and another walking behind. Maybe so I couldn't run, but what would be the point? They would only get me again. They rarely spoke to me, they just chatted and laughed with each other. It was so inhuman – they simply marched me to a room or a flat, knowing what they were taking me to, acting as if it was the most natural thing in the world. I guess for them, it was.

Gordon had been telling me how to dress until he disappeared from the scene – it was either my old school uniform or things he wanted me to wear, normally the sluttier the better. I kept those clothes hidden away in a bag but when these new men turned up, they didn't care. It was the white men who wanted me to look like a slut or a schoolgirl, or a combination of both. The Pakistani men weren't bothered – for them, treating me like shit was the main thing, it seemed. The white men – well, I think it was acting out pornographic fantasies, whereas for the others it was all about hating white women and girls. The white men wanted a schoolgirl, the Pakistani men just wanted to hurt a white girl – to them she was trash anyway.

Meanwhile the sexual acts were getting worse – it all became more violent, with many of the men wanting to tie me up and whip me. I never had any warning that they might want that but then it wasn't something I looked out for – I expected the same sort of thing as before. I can't recall the face of the first one who did it. There was one man who liked to use tight leather to tie me to the bed so my arms couldn't move. He had some sort of attachment on the leather that could tighten up the parts holding me in place but I couldn't see the details – my hands would be behind my back as I knelt down on the floor.

'Sit down, on your knees! Stay still, don't move!' he would snap at me.

He was a horrible man and I dreaded any time he walked in the room. The thing was, I never knew who would be there or what they would want. When the men who now owned me collected me, they would take me in, usually to a flat, and I would know that I wouldn't be getting out until they were done. I'd have no say – I just had to get through the production line.

There was one particular flat with a room and a doorway into it that I can see in my mind's eye even now. The bedroom had been turned into a living room and always there were about eight men in there. I'd be put in this bedroom and one after the other they would all come in. I'd been taken there before I'd moved to the hostel too, when I lived at home.

They were verbally abusive too, straight away. This way they operated was the biggest change; it was quite literally one after the other, a whole line of them. I wasn't even allowed to get off that bed. Soon I went from one man per visit to about four and that was horrible enough but then it went up to about eight.

These men were my abusers now and they were all Pakistani without exception.

'Kafir girl,' they would taunt me, 'kafir girl, you are white trash.'

'Slut, white slut.'

'White bitch, white whore, white cunt.'

All of it – not just about me being a woman, a young woman, but being a *white* woman; being different to them, being less than them because of my colour. To me that's the biggest irony of all. Whenever I've told anyone about it, they cry 'Racist!' but these men never said a word to me without it being loaded with racial abuse.

I remember so many of them saying, 'We are allowed to do this in our culture' – they were allowed to rape me, they said, because it didn't count. In other words, *I* didn't count. I'd say to every white woman reading this, never doubt what a group of these men might be thinking about you and saying about you. It was made clear to me from the start that I was seen as trash and that it was fine to think of me in that way: I was nothing to them, I wasn't even human. If you walk past a group of these men on the street and their eyes follow you and you hear them laugh, they might be telling each other what they would like to do to a filthy white bitch like you. And they're telling themselves and each other that this is 'allowed', because to them you are nothing, you are lower than the shit on their shoes.

It was around this time that I was taken to a different house to the usual ones. They were always around the same streets, around a mosque, in what was almost a completely Muslim area. It's not a good idea for any white woman to be there, nothing good would ever come of it.

These men took me to a flat, and in it were two men. I wanted to leave immediately – there was something I didn't like, something I just sensed was worse than usual.

By now, I had started to carry a blade for self-harming, a Stanley knife blade, so I pulled it out on one of them. One of the men moved to block the door, someone I'd never seen before, so I pulled the blade and held it up with all of the strength I could manage, saying, 'Fuckin' let me go!' But he just reached over and caught my hand, squeezing my fingers around the very blade I had thought might give me some protection. I didn't argue after that – I've blocked the rest of that out, but I know I didn't go for treatment.

It was getting worse, that's for sure. I needed to find a way out, and I really didn't think there was anyone who could help me – but I knew now that I would grab the chance if it ever came.

CHAPTER 6

you belong to us

I stayed in the hostel for a few months. It was full of people like me, all lost and looking for a way out. But it wasn't a place we were ever going to find sanctuary.

Down the hall there was a couple called Fatima and Neil, both of them junkies. She was mixed-race and he was white. They just turned up one day and told me that I would work for them – I never did but they still bothered me. She once even held a knife to my stomach.

Everyone in the hostel knew what was happening, I think. Often I wondered if Fatima had been a girl like me, if she'd been used too, and that was why she was so cruel to others who were also going through it.

I always wanted to trust the women though. I always wanted them to save me, but I think they were all in a pretty bad situation too. I remember one, Noor, who was married to this vile bloke called Kevin. She was in her forties and I wondered if I would end up like her one day and whether that would be a life I could deal with. They actually lived there with their little boy who spent his life sitting in the living room while only God knows what went on – he must have only been about four or five, sitting there, watching a DVD while his parents did that. Much later, I bumped into them and Kevin said, 'My son really fancies you. He's sixteen soon, will you look after him?' I didn't of course, but it was a sickening thought.

Luckily, I wasn't there long. Living in the hostel was just compounding everything and certainly didn't feel anything like a 'home' so my parents decided that I should move into a bedsit. After everything that had happened in the last few months, with what they saw as my 'acting out', they were trying to help, which was nice of them, but the bedsit was in a very bad area. I don't think they realised at the time, but it was the typical working girl sort of place you can all probably imagine.

That's about the time I met Kashif. I can't remember who I met him through, but it may have been his sister, Zainab, as she was always hanging around, looking for more youngsters to siphon off to the men she knew. Zainab and Kashif were both drug addicts and they would do anything for their next hit, but Kashif was actually always nice to me. He never laid a finger on me and would give me food from the kebab shop he ran which was only five minutes' walk from the bedsit.

It wasn't long before Kashif introduced me to a man who called himself 'The Boss'. I never knew his real name but I remember his face to this day. When I say Kashif was 'nice', I mean that was only because he didn't rape me – he still facilitated with others and, actually, The Boss was absolutely horrific.

Kashif would ring me to go to the kebab shop and when I got there The Boss would be waiting for me. I think he had paid to use me as well, as I started to be given to a new group of men at that time too.

I was still self-harming and there were visible signs of

the cutting I was doing, all over my body. In that group was one man who wasn't at all bothered by this fact. None of them really cared, they just ignored it, but this particular man (I've no idea what he was called) was clearly excited by it.

As soon as I took my clothes off and he saw the scars, old and new, he said, 'Let me do it!'

'Do *what*?' I asked, wearily.

'Let me do *that*,' he said, pointing to my marked skin. 'Let me cut you.'

'You want to cut me?' I asked, still able to feel shocked by such a suggestion.

'Yes! *Yes*! *Bloodplay* – let us do bloodplay!' he shouted.

I'd never heard of it before and he did cut me a bit. To be honest, it sounds fucked up, but I didn't really care at that point – I was drinking a lot to cope, which made things a bit more bearable; the men (the good Muslim men who were never supposed to go anywhere near alcohol but who drank vodka all day) gave it to me. Every now and again I'd be given money for underwear but they mainly gave me a lot of alcohol.

My dad, unknowingly, sometimes bought me

alcohol too. I'd pop home every now and then, always hoping they'd see what was really going on, always hoping they'd save me. I think he must have realised something was going on but I don't know how much. Looking back, I do wonder why he did that though – surely it would have been better to try and deal with what was going on, rather than give me booze? Sam, my younger brother, was furious when he realised. He wanted in on the act too, in typical sibling rivalry style – I doubt he'd have been so keen if he'd known why I was getting it.

'You let Caitlin have it but not me,' he protested.

'Well, she needs it, she's having a rough time,' replied Dad.

He didn't know the half of it.

I'd had three suicide attempts by this point, alone in my grotty bedsit, but I have largely blocked those out. It's only when I read my medical notes now that I even know some things have happened. All I remember of my first overdose was that I took a load of paracetamol washed down with Malibu. I was hoping I wouldn't wake up. I was so sick, but I was really just learning how to do it – I never went to hospital for any of those three attempts. I've done it so many times, but I never got that right either.

I do know that when I tried, my mind would keep drifting back to Gordon and what had started it all. I knew by then that the man who had 'bought' me from him was called Hassan and he had a sidekick called Ali. They always seemed to be together – the only time they weren't was when Hassan went back home to Pakistan. He did this fairly regularly and I was told by someone it was because he was a politician there. These memories would go round and round in my head. I couldn't get out of my mind the time that Hassan had first cornered me when he saw me walking home one evening. He took my phone to add his number to my contacts list and to allow him to get mine – it was after this that Gordon pretty much disappeared and I wondered if I'd been sold.

I think I was, I really do – I don't see why Gordon would just disappear if not. Why would he? He had an interest in me, he was making money, I assume, and it was very sudden. My relief at him going proved short-lived, considering how things had spiralled since then.

By now, just seventeen, the police had told me I

was a known prostitute and they had put me on their system. Their psychiatrist said it was imaginary and I'd had a breakdown. One of the few people who has ever tried to help me was a social worker assigned to me around this time. She even tried to tell the police what was happening too, but I was just one of many on her list, another messed-up girl who they ignored. No one believed my story, it seemed, and so when my next suicide attempt didn't work, I'd decided that I wanted to kill Gordon.

I took a knife with me after I called to say that I wanted to meet him in a park, very late, when it was extremely dark. I had every intention of stabbing him but I lost my shit completely. I don't have much memory of that night – I was being used by the Pakistani men but it was Gordon I wanted to go back and kill, even though I hadn't heard from him in a while. He was the one who had started it all off after all. I was in a bad way, with these terrible thoughts swirling my mind; I was trapped.

* * *

When Hassan – and Ali – controlled me, it was a proper

production line. They would tell me that I belonged to them, that I had no say in matters, and they were right. One after the other they would wait for me – waiting their turn. They didn't even care if other men watched while they raped me; it seemed almost a bonding thing for them. I don't even remember them all. I got in taxis thinking it was safe and then they'd say to me, as if we were friends, 'Oh, you don't remember me, do you?' Then I'd think, 'Oh fuck, you were one of them too.'

I was getting a lot of STDs by now, which caused me a lot of physical pain, not that it stopped the abuse – I would keep going back to the clinic on my own to get the treatment but it wouldn't work as I was still seeing so many men. The clinic actually told me one of the diseases solely originates from Pakistan, but nothing was ever done about it, no one expressed any real concern. These men were presumably having unprotected sex with their wives too.

Hassan told me he had a building business and sometimes he would give me to some of his builders as a bonus if they had worked well. There was never hot water or even running water in those places, not even toilet paper for me to mop myself up afterwards. They always had time to get a bed in there though. It seemed they had no concern they would ever be caught to face justice and I was starting to join it all up; they were untouchable somehow.

For the next year it was the same old shit – new men all the time, different days. Many were local but some were visiting, some didn't speak English at all but they were friends of the men who already abused me. I wonder what those conversations were like – did they ask the family they were visiting if they knew of a teenager they could rape, or was I offered up as a welcoming gift? Did they discuss me, compare what they did? It beggars belief.

Hassan was certainly very keen on making me see his friends and visiting family. One day he told me, 'I have some special friends over from India, we're going to have a party.'

Those words always struck the fear of God into me – not because of what they would do to me, I was almost numb to that, but because there would be other girls and I knew that Hassan liked them young, *very* young. He particularly liked a girl called Becca, who couldn't have been much more than twelve years old. She was from a children's home and they went for her whenever they wanted because they knew they could, I suppose. The home was eventually shut down a few years later, probably because I'd heard that the people running the place were complicit in it all, but not before a lot of damage was done to a lot of children. I know there was a social worker who had tried to do something about it, but no one listened to her at the time either.

Hassan also frequently used another young girl from the same home called Hayley – she was maybe a year older than Becca and they were both tiny little things, so young and vulnerable.

I spoke to Becca quite a lot and felt protective of both of them; in fact, I'd even spoken out on one occasion, which, as you know, wasn't like me at all. We had all been taken to Watford one day and Becca was getting quite upset as she had to be back for curfew. It was 1am by this point and she was panicking. We had been in a hotel for the day, all three of us, being used by one man after another, then we were taken to a car park, where they just waited in their vehicles until it was their turn for one of us. There were so many of them and one of the guys slapped Becca as she was crying so much.

I'm not proud of myself, but I called him a 'Paki cunt'. I was so outraged, but I got in big trouble for that. I knew what I was doing, though: if I did that, the man would concentrate on hitting me instead and leave her alone. That night I got a good hiding but at least he didn't go back to Becca.

So when Hassan told me that there would be a party for his friends, I just knew Becca would be there: she was his prized girl, the youngest one, the smallest one, the one he paraded as proof of his absolute power and control. These parties would always be in a house – this one was in a nice place, quite big and nicely decorated too.

There were quite a few guys downstairs with their drinks and their food. I couldn't stand it – the smell of it, the smell of *them*. Hassan always brought the food and the drink. He liked Blue Nun, the cheap white wine – he always had lots of that as well as vodka. We were plied with it. There would be two girls waiting downstairs and one upstairs and they would pick whichever girl they wanted and do what they wanted. It was one at a time in the bedroom while the others waited. That must have been a power thing – keep two of us waiting while we knew what was happening to the other. *What was worse, waiting or the reality?* They could easily have used another room – I doubt they thought we had the strength to make a run for it either.

On that occasion, I just knew Hassan had something planned, but I didn't know what. While the other girls were being used, he kept Becca and Hayley and me in a room together with the other men. There was lots of laughter, a real party atmosphere – for *them*.

'Now, girls,' he announced, to an audience of 'friends', 'tonight is your lucky night.'

They all cheered as we sat there – lambs to the slaughter.

'Tonight, all three of you filthy white whores will be delighted to know that you have all been privileged to be chosen by *me*!'

There was whooping and more cheering, and he was clapped on the back. Meanwhile we just sat there, dead to the world. We'd already been plied with alcohol, forcing it down our throats if we wouldn't drink it – and some pills, exactly what they were I don't know

– so there wouldn't have been much of a response anyway. We knew we would have to take whatever it was. I could feel Becca starting to shake next to me and so I tried to comfort her a little by holding her hand as surreptitiously as possible.

'*Yes*!' shouted Hassan with glee. 'Let's have our own party!'

And with that, the men roughly pushed all three of us on our feet as it dawned on me what was happening: a foursome. He wanted a foursome of him, me, and two children. As they marched us upstairs, Hassan at the front as if he was some sort of emperor, a man worthy of reverence rather than a paedophile and rapist, a man who was thought of as respectable, I felt sick.

When we got to the bedroom door, they pushed us in and I remember him shouting, 'Wait your turn, gentlemen! Maybe there will be some left after Hassan has finished – who knows?'

He told us what to do – he had to, we were clueless. It was so awkward, so disgusting. The other girls were just twelve or thirteen and we were all having to 'pleasure' this hideous man as if we were enjoying it, like we'd chosen to be there. I'd never had to do this before and I felt so bad about it, those girls. I hated myself for being part of it, and I still feel shameful to this day.

Hassan used the word 'party' liberally. Whenever he had people visiting, more often men who couldn't speak English, they were the visitors to be indulged and we were just entertainment, we were dehumanised. I'm sure they didn't even think of it as rape, they just felt permitted to do this.

And these 'parties' weren't just in flats and houses. There was also a budget hotel we were taken to that was really isolated. The rooms are like a prison, with concrete walls, and they would book them out for days and keep girls there the whole time. The hotel must have just been happy to get some business, no one ever seemed to notice.

Becca was one of these girls and when she was let out, she was taken to a detention centre for her safety so someone somewhere obviously knew what was happening. I think a lot of people did actually, they just didn't want to address it – what could they really prove anyway?

I was once taken to a massive Tesco to buy things

for a 'party' and I don't know what made me do it that day, but I just couldn't face going back with them. So I plucked up the courage to speak to the store security guard.

I said, 'I have to go back to a hotel with these guys – but I don't want to. Is there any way I can get out without using the front door?'

To his credit, he didn't even question me – maybe he'd seen them before, perhaps he'd heard what was going on in the area. Whatever it was, he took me to a staff exit away from the public area and I breathed a sigh of relief as I waited a little while so I could work out my bearings. I shouldn't have waited at all – they came and found me straight away as it turned out they'd been watching me and when I didn't come out of the main exit they came straight round the block as they knew there was only one other way I could have got out.

These men all drank so much, and they made me drink so much too. It numbed me but it also meant I could never escape – they'd always find me anyway. At certain times of the afternoon they would nip out to go to the Mosque, not all of them, just some, and they would come back afterwards. The ones who lived in this country would speak English at times – 'I'm going to Mosque now, I'll be back soon. You wait here, kafir girl,' they would say. So, off they would go. They would pray, they would be good religious men – then they would come back and rape me again for the day.

The worst thing was not knowing what they would want – I always worried what they would come up with next. To be honest, I hated it most when the other girls were involved because they were so young. When we had to pick them up, I felt awful – I wished they'd just gone for older ones. Becca, in particular, was so very young.

They never wanted me to pretend I was enjoying it – for them it was straight on the bed, do this, do that, we don't really care. The vulgar truth is, I was just a hole to them. Every now and again I would get £10 – not a lot, not often. It was as if they were doing me a huge favour. I knew by now that most of the taxi companies were a part of it early on as they drove them and took me there. These men seemed particularly fearless – they would just pick the girls they knew off the streets, mainly girls from care homes or hostels. They seemed to think they would never be touched for it, and neither did I.

CHAPTER 7

a day

It all blends into itself. Everything is the same; nothing changes. More men, more pain – more hell.

A typical day? This is me... This is me in a room. I'm waiting – I was either waiting or it was happening. I'd get picked up from wherever I was; I'd be taken through the side door into what was like a waiting room in the house. They didn't even bother to register when I came in, or look at me properly. One time, I was sat on a little sofa and there was a bed to the side and a few chairs around a coffee table – although I could see what it was for, it wasn't like a proper home: it's there for only one reason.

They are all talking in their own language, which is scary. You're a stranger. A stranger waiting for other strangers to do whatever they want and you can't even understand what they're saying but you know, you just *know*, it's about you – they laugh, they point, they look at you.

They're saying what they always say, even if it's in another language. Then, sometimes, they speak in English so you will hear it.

Cunt.

White trash.

Slut.

White whore.

Just the same things as ever. White noise. That's funny... White, white, white.

When I arrive there's another girl there – they're waiting to use the room with me when she's done. As if she has any choice. When *they're* done. They like to have more than one there at a time. Control. Power. They let you know that they can do what they want with as many as they want: not just you, you're just one of many. Her hell is *your* hell – you're all nothing, you're all disposable. There have been girls before you and there will be girls after you.

Just another girl.

Just another day.

Sometimes, something will be different. I wait there for the other girl to be done and for the room to be available for me.

Hurry up; hurry up and take turns in raping me. Let's get this over with so we can do it all again the next time, and the next time and the next time…

They're talking, laughing. One man is shoved playfully in the arm by another man – they are winding him up, I think. They look at me, they laugh: it would appear that I'm hilarious. The man leans over to a bag, a black holdall at the side of him. It looks like the sort of bag that workmen carry with their tools inside. They're finding this really funny.

He reaches inside.

I'm watching out of the corner of my eye, not directly, not wishing to engage. If this is for me, if they're waiting on my response, they won't get it. I'm dead inside, and I try to be dead on the outside too. But he reaches in and in a flash, he's over at the side of me and there's something in his hand and he's pressing it against my knee…

...and it's a drill.

It's a fucking drill.

He removes it from my skin slightly when I flinch at the touch then he presses the button and it whirrs, it whirrs, and they're finding this the funniest thing in the world. The white trash girl they all rape and their friend pressing an electric drill against her knee. He's on one side, and another man is on the other side, and they're not bothered about me, I'm just there. But then I see the look in his eye and it's pure hatred. He despises me – they all do – but this cuts through the laughter they're all enjoying together and I know he's deciding: he's deciding whether it's worth it. Would he get away with it? Could he press the button harder, push it into my knee, feel the bone shatter, see the blood flow?

Would he face any repercussions at all?

I don't think he would – they would cover up for him. I think they'd bury me if they had to, but he thinks twice and decides against it. He keeps pressing the button as he withdraws the drill, each time making me flinch, but the moment has passed. For now I'll just be raped.

Just the usual for today, thanks.

When I'm there, when it's just another day, they touch me all the time when I'm on the sofa between them, waiting. It doesn't even affect the flow of their conversation. They paw me, touching my legs, my breasts, between my legs. Nothing is private, nothing is forbidden, and I just sit there; I let them.

I zone out.

I'm not wearing any make-up, I'm not dolled up. I have a short skirt on – they need access, after all – but this isn't some happy hooker myth, I'm just a vessel. There are always more men coming into the room all the time, talking and laughing, never bothering about me really, I'm just there for them. While they talk to each other and they touch me, it's almost as if it's an afterthought. Sometimes, I think they're talking about me but they don't want me to hear. They look at me every so often and keep to their own language, even lowering their own voices despite me not knowing a word of it. There are about eight men, and I always think, *am I to deal with them all?*

There is one man sitting there and I know him.

Tariq.

I know Tariq.

He's staring at me – he will be one of them today but it won't be as bad as it's been before with him, because there are others here and I think they'll stop him if he tries to do what he's said he will do.

One day, Tariq took me to a flat on his own, which was unusual. He held a knife to my throat while he was on top of me and said, 'I'm going to put you under my floorboards, white bitch, and no one will know as I'm going to Pakistan in a week.' I wasn't that scared as by then I was beyond caring, but looking back, I know that given the chance he would go further than he should; he wouldn't stop at rape. If he saw me in town he'd stalk me, following me through all the shops, staring at me from a distance even if I was with someone. He didn't go to Pakistan after all – he's still here, but any of them could go at any time if they had to. They have a place to run, a place to hide; they're very different from me. He's in the queue today – I'll have to deal with Tariq.

In that room they are all different ages, shapes and sizes, all of them showing the signs of having a good life. They're in their thirties, forties, fifties, sixties – maybe some in their seventies. This need they have, this wish to do these things, is like generational glue. I bring them all together with my nasty, filthy, broken little body. These men are pillars of their community, mostly builders and taxi drivers, business owners and family men.

The girl is done with now. They all move as she is brought out and leaves – she walks out silently, passively, just like I do. There are no chains or padlocks on the door, no one is holding a gun to our heads; they control us much more effectively than that.

This is what happens, this is what *always* happens. I'm taken into the room by one man – which one? To me they are all the same.

'Take off your clothes,' he says.

'Get on the bed,' he tells me.

I know these things. He doesn't have to tell me, but it's part of it, part of the ritual, the never-endingness of it all.

I look at the windows while I wait. They're locked. Old ones, sash and case, but they're either painted over in some flats or locked as in this one. I couldn't have climbed out anyway, but those windows are probably the only restrictions.

As that man leaves, another man comes in the room, does what he wants to do, goes. Even as he's going out, someone else is coming in. Sometimes they will come back again – eight of them doesn't necessarily mean eight times. And it won't necessarily be once today – I might have to come back in the evening, if they come for me.

Most of this batch like the same thing – they want rape and oral sex, they all want that. I once had a guy who brought some liquid with him, with Arabic writing on the bottle. I have no idea what it was, but he poured it on me and it really hurt. He poured it all over my private parts then he raped me; it was horrible. Is it OK to say that, to say it was horrible? It seems such a small word for what happened.

Horrible.

Nasty.

Painful.

Degrading.

Of course it was, of course it was all of those things – but I want new words. New words that will pull together what it feels like to be small and young and alone, to feel that you're worthless and wrecked for life, that this will never end and no one will ever love you or want you in a normal way ever again.

There are no words though, are there? 'Horrible' will have to do.

When the 'horrible' is over – although I might have to come back – I get up from the floor or the bed. Now this is disgusting but I have to say it: I am full of them. It falls out of me, what they have left in me. They don't use protection and I can taste them, feel them. What they have deposited in me coats my mouth and fills between my legs. It's running down those legs that they have pushed apart, it's crusting on the edges of my lips where they forced my mouth open to do what they wanted to do over and over again.

You'll despise me for this, won't you?

You'll be reading this, and you'll probably have had a nice life, a good life, and you'll think, *why did she allow that? Why did she allow so many? Why did she allow so much of it?*

Maybe you'll remember the windows were locked, but perhaps you'll also remember that the door wasn't locked much more clearly.

I wouldn't have let them do that, you'll think (unless you've been through it too). And, do you know what?

Sometimes I feel that way too. I think that it would only be a certain type of person – a person like *me* – who would have let them force my legs open, force my mouth open, say filthy things to me, degrade and abuse me, because, after all, I'm shit.

And you're not.

So, shit, broken me, let them do what they wanted, then I got up, walked out and left without saying a word. Sometimes I would see the next girl, sometimes I would care. Sometimes I wouldn't even know where I was until I was at the bedsit.

Then I'd wait. Maybe go back again that night. Maybe do it all over again. Just wait…

Just wait.

CHAPTER 8

please, let me go

Have you ever felt fear so deep in your chest that you feel like you're always on the edge of a panic attack, but without the physical panic? You can't breathe but you're suffocating. Your skin itches so much, it's aching to be broken. You feel so dirty that you want to bleed until you're clean. So many things running through your head that leave you with a constant feeling of nausea – you can't sleep but you have so much shame and self-loathing that you want to sleep forever. Have you ever felt any of that? I feel all of that, I have since the start and I still do. I don't know how to make it go away, I never have – I'm trapped in this tainted body for my entire life, yet another choice I don't have. It's almost as if their handprints are visible over my body, and no matter how much I scrub and scrub, I can't get them off. I think I'll always feel them in me, on me, around me.

After a year or so, it was all becoming unbearable with no sense that there would ever be any way out – then, incredibly, something changed.

While I was living in the bedsit, Mum and Dad realised that nothing was getting any better. I guess they saw the superficial stuff – I was drinking a lot, there were suicide attempts, and I was self-harming. They thought I was 'wild' and, even if that wasn't quite the truth, at least it made them take some action.

Dad had a cousin called Mary who lived in Australia and now, when I was still just eighteen, they decided that three months with her might 'bring me to my senses', as they called it. They paid for it all, and I think they really thought it would help me to make – and choose – a new life. I was so relieved. They truly had no idea. I was sure it would be good to break away too and I clung to the idea, although I still didn't mention anything to my parents about what I was enduring despite the fact that I was still in the clutches of those men right up until the day before I left.

They had no idea I was planning to leave, and I can only imagine how they reacted when they came to my bedsit and realised I wasn't there anymore.

In fact, on my last night in the country and in their clutches, I remember lying there thinking, 'You'll never touch me again.'

Dad actually flew over with me and stayed with Mary and her family for two weeks. I'd only met her once before and I didn't really know much about her – I wish I had. The plan was that I was to live there with her and try and establish a 'normal' life, but Mary was completely unstable. She supposedly had a counselling degree but to me it seemed she was more in need of counselling than any of her clients could have been. She seemed nice enough when Dad was there though, and I was just so happy to be far far away, so it took me a while to really see it.

Mary had three kids including a daughter, Jade, who was a little bit older than me and I got on well with her, but to be honest, even from the start, I avoided Mary as much as possible. I think Dad must have told her what was going on with me – well, as much as he knew or would admit to – and she had decided I would be a project for her. She would have fainted if she'd known the truth.

Mary lived in a lovely house in Melbourne, although to Australians it would probably be seen as quite a rough area. After Dad went back to England, I tried to settle in and actually I did enjoy being with Mary's kids, especially Jade, but I think I was too damaged by this point, too far gone for anything to help. I was still self-harming and it seemed I couldn't get out of it – I did it every day with blades and I was also throwing up my food. Mary knew, as she could see and hear me, but I didn't want to confide in her.

I was also acting out sexually – I guess that was all I knew and, in Australia, I told myself it was my choice – which I'd never had before. I don't know why I did it; even now I feel very uncomfortable with men touching me in any way. Disassociation? Control? I was all over the place. I went with someone in a public pool and was subsequently banned, so I was grounded for that. Looking back on it now, I was awful, I really was. But because I was choosing for the first time and it was all I knew, I thought that was OK. I didn't like it though. I've never enjoyed sex, even now I find it painful – I don't like it one little bit.

Mary was strict with me and I think she was probably right to try and rein me in, but back then, I'd been through so much, so my approach was 'Fuck off, you've no idea what I've been through'. She wasn't the calmest person in the world either, to put it mildly, so we just rubbed each other up the wrong way. In fact, she lied even when it was easier to tell the truth and that just made me want to be naughtier. She even told my parents that I was pregnant when I wasn't, and accused me of emailing a man to hook up despite the fact I didn't even have an email address back then. She tried to counsel me, but I didn't want to know or talk to her – she knew some things about me that I'd never told her so Mum or Dad must have told her, but they didn't know the full story anyway and they'd been lying to themselves for so long that, by now, I was really angry that they felt they had the right to try and palm me off to this madwoman who just saw me as a project for her own ends.

Mary made me write down three things that would make me happy but when I wrote down materialistic things, she went mad. If I'd really written what I wanted, she wouldn't have been able to cope. I'd have liked men to stop raping me, men to stop forcing me to have sex on demand, and men to leave me alone. How would you have achieved that, Mary, with your little crystals and your yoga?

For something I'd felt was finally going to be my escape, the whole experience just ended up making things so much worse. I'd been desperate for help for so long, but this was just pushing me further and further away.

In the end, I was only in Australia for three months before I went back home. I truly never thought that I would have chosen to come back but if I couldn't live with and be supported by Mary then I didn't have a choice. I didn't have any money and I wasn't legally allowed to work there. Initially I'd hoped to apply for a visa, but the problems with Mary were just too big and I could also see that my own behaviour was appalling. Yes, I was choosing to do these things but I must have been pretty messed-up in the first place for it all to seem like good options.

So, I went back home – I went back to it all, and almost immediately they got me. It was as if I'd never been away. They spotted me in the street and I was straight back to that terrified, conditioned little girl who couldn't say 'no', who thought that this was what she deserved. This time around things were even worse because I'd proved to myself that I could screw up even when given a chance. I'd been so desperate to escape and then when I'd been given the opportunity, I'd blown it. So, I felt I deserved this: I deserved to go back to it.

***

Nothing had changed: same men, same old shit again. They were scary as well – one of them threatened to pour acid over me, another said he would shove it down my throat, one of them cornered me against a wall and said I had to do whatever he wanted. Even now, I would get in the car if they told me to – they terrified me.

As I lay there one day, I whispered to myself, 'Please, let me go, please let me go, please let me go…' I was trapped. As surely as if they had locked me in that room and thrown away the key, I was trapped. I could no more get up and walk out than I could fly to the moon. These men had completely broken me and I was utterly helpless. I'd been raped so many times, abused by hundreds, if not thousands of men; I was emotionally and psychologically shattered to the extent that they could have left every door open and it would have made no difference. In fact, it *did* make no difference: I walked the streets, I went home to my parents' house most nights. And I always came back – they *always* brought me back. I accepted it all, because not only was I nothing to them, I was also nothing to myself.

But I knew that if I stayed there, the only real place I knew, I'd never escape. I needed to get away again. I kept thinking about my lost chance, about how I'd missed the possibility of a new life in Australia and I was desperate to go back almost as soon as I returned to the UK. Of course I knew I could never stay with Mary again, but surely there was another way? I knew these guys were making a lot of money from me as I saw it change hands, but I had no money of my own and my parents were furious with me because the stay with

Mary hadn't worked out so they wouldn't be funding another trip.

I had to find another option so I did what I thought I'd never do.

I put myself on the streets.

Why not? It couldn't be any worse and at least I'd have some control. Just as I told myself in Australia, at least it would be my decision and by now I really felt that it was all I knew. I already knew how the other girls 'worked' and it would get me the money to leave.

In the end I only managed a couple of times: I was terrified, and I thought that if the men found out, their abusive threats might become a reality.

This was the early 2000s and the social side of the internet was booming. I'd been in online chat rooms by now, just trying to find people to have normal conversations with; for me it was a means of escape and control, even if it was only in the virtual world. But there were a lot of creeps out there.

I started to wonder whether it could help me though – could I find someone who would help me get to Australia and secure a visa so that I could stay there permanently? It sounds manipulative, but I was desperate. You have to understand that when you've been abused from such a young age, everything about your world view is skewed. I didn't think anyone could be trusted and I didn't really believe that I deserved good things. My body was wrecked and I was almost immune to the horrific things men wanted to do to me, so if that was my only currency, so be it. It seemed to be all men wanted to trade in anyway.

In one of the chatrooms, I'd actually been talking to an Australian guy anyway – Vernon was in Melbourne, just like Mary, so there was that connection. It wasn't any sort of real relationship and we didn't have cybersex or anything like that, but I knew he liked me. Maybe I reeled him in, maybe he did the same to me, who knows? I didn't know real boundaries of relationships anyway. Whatever it was, the upshot was that he offered to pay for me to fly out to meet him. Even after everything I've said, I never truly believed I would take him up on it until I realised I was never going to get the money together myself so I needed to just go for it. I decided I would get there and stay with my cousin Jade who had moved into her own flat.

So Vernon sent the money for me to get a ticket –

God, how naïve was I? Looking back, I really thought I was in control. I'd grown up the hard way – what problem could I possibly have with just another man? I told my parents I was going to stay with a guy off the internet, but by now, I'd let them down so much that it seemed to me they didn't really care. So I bought a return ticket as you couldn't get into the country without one; you had to prove that you planned to leave again and not become an 'illegal'. I barely remember getting ready for that trip, or the flight itself.

Just over six months since I'd last been there, I was back in Melbourne.

***

Vernon met me at the airport. I'd seen a genuine pic of him; he hadn't tried to hide that he was just a regular bloke. He was about late 20s, short, a bit podgy – and he lived with his mum. The plan was that I would stay with him (I knew I was only going to do that for a few days though, then I would go to Jade, although he didn't know that). Bizarrely, Vernon's mum seemed fine about his English friend coming to stay, and although he expected me to be his girlfriend, I didn't see that as a problem. I thought, *I'll do what it takes, I don't care.* What was one more man after all?

So he took my back to his mum's house and she was really nice to me. I had a separate room though as she was very strict. I might have been Vernon's new girlfriend from England but she didn't want any funny business so when she went to bed I went to his room and did whatever he wanted me to do. What else would I do? I didn't know anything else. It seemed Vernon couldn't believe his luck, and within forty-eight hours, he wanted us to get married. By now, I'd seen his 'shed' that he was so proud of, which was completely decorated in Nazi memorabilia and swastikas, so marriage definitely wasn't included in any plans of mine and it never had been. In fact, I quickly began to see that he was very controlling. He hated me talking to anyone, even his mum, and my plans to run away to Jade's were coming to nothing as he kept me in his sight at all times. Jade didn't even know I was in the country!

One day, a couple of weeks after I'd arrived, Vernon announced that we were going to a local restaurant to meet some friends of his. The words 'friends' struck terror in me as it took me back, but there was no real reason to fear this. He said there was someone who could help me get my visa as he knew that was what my ultimate aim was. We turned up to meet a young woman called Jodie, whose boyfriend was the manager there. Jodie was really friendly and soon put me at ease. She said that she had arranged for an older couple to join us as they were experts in visa applications. I'd told Vernon that I was in a bit of trouble back home but I hadn't really gone into too much detail. However, given that I'd been stupid enough to fly across the world to meet a complete stranger and was now having sex with him, I guess everyone could have guessed what sort of trouble I was in. I think I may have said that some guys had made me do some things I didn't want to do, but I certainly hadn't told anyone the true horror of it. I now know that in telling him even that, I was giving him some power. That was stupid of me, so very stupid.

When the couple arrived, they seemed very nice. 'Harry and Gretchen will get you everything you need,' said Vernon, and I believed him. I completely fell for it. The thing was, I knew the visa situation was very strict in Australia and Vernon, as well as Jodie and her boyfriend, were telling me that this couple knew powerful people who could help. And they were right – they *did* know some powerful people, but they also seemed to see me as someone who would just be a pawn in whatever game they decided to play.

I told myself that Harry and Gretchen were just nice people and that I shouldn't always be so suspicious. And they did seem that way to start with. Gretchen was actually really sweet. I still find it hard to dislike her even now. In fact, I miss her, and that is really fucked up. To be honest, as soon as I met them and they promised to help, I saw them as my way out. But Vernon didn't like it at all.

'Why can't you carry on staying with me?' he asked. The truth was, I was going to work for them. To pay them back for their help, and to earn a bit of money for myself, they had offered me a job as a receptionist.

I'm embarrassed to tell this part of my story because every single person reading this book will know what's coming. Every single person will see the writing on the wall. But me? Foolish, broken Caitlin? No, I just saw a receptionist job and a potential visa.

And where was the receptionist's job?

In a fucking brothel.

I must have had *IDIOT* written all over me.

From the start Harry and Gretchen had been quite open with me about the sort of business they ran and it turned out that Jodie was one of their 'girls'. They had a few businesses, but this was their main source of income. Although they presented it as a massage parlour, everyone knew what it was.

'All our girls are so happy,' Gretchen told me. 'We're just like one big, happy family. They can come and go when they like, and they earn really good money.'

So I lapped it all up. I truly believed the whole Dolly Parton *The Best Little Whorehouse in Texas* romanticised vision. It would be clean and I would have a choice – and that choice was to be the receptionist. In exchange, they would help me get a visa.

'We know a politician.' Harry explained to me. 'He's a very good friend of ours. You work with us, he'll know you're a good girl, and he'll be more than happy to help you.'

It all seemed much better than at home. Yes, I'd be working in a brothel but I wouldn't be selling myself. It didn't even really bother me that other young women would be, because Gretchen seemed so lovely and she had sold me this notion that it was all consensual. I can't believe I fell for it, but I did. I guess my mind was just so warped by what I'd already been through that I was very easily manipulated – and they were experts.

I was still staying with Vernon and travelled in every day, even though the plan was for me to stay with the couple eventually. I've no idea what Vernon told his mum, but I think she just thought it was good that I had a job and was getting 'settled'. Harry or his driver, Doug, would call for me and take me there. Looking back, I think they were waiting to see how trusting I was.

They must have been delighted.

I couldn't have been more of a gullible fool if I'd tried.

CHAPTER 9

safe haven

On the first day, it seemed fine. Harry and Gretchen were in a room when I got there, a waiting room with a big fish tank, bright and clean. There was a desk for me and rooms out the back where the 'girls' worked. In fact, it stayed fine for a week or so, then Gretchen told me that they had a spare room for me so I could move in. I was keen to get away from Vernon as he was an oddball, so I saw this as a safe haven. It would be where I would get my visa and after that I could do whatever I wanted. I didn't plan to work there forever, I would be able to recreate myself once I had residency, just as I'd hoped.

Every cliché you have ever heard came at me as soon as I did move in.

Harry needed to take my passport because it was required for the application.

Harry needed to take my mobile phone because it would be distracting while I worked.

Harry needed to send his driver Doug with me every time I left the building to make sure I was safe.

They controlled me from the start, and I just went along with it, because, after all, I was the girl who never said 'no'.

It all changed so fast. Once Harry and Gretchen gave me a spare room, they told me I would have to pay board but they never said how much, they just said they would deduct it from my wages. Harry said I needed to pull my weight a bit once I lived there. I needed to make more money. 'You need to pay this and this and this,' he'd tell me, meaning all the visa costs and lots of other things he tried to confuse me about, but I don't think they were real.

It wasn't long before they both told me that I would have to work there as one of their 'girls'. 'It won't be often,' Gretchen explained, 'it's just that you're costing us so much and we really do want to help you.' *I'd done it before*, I told myself – *how bad could it be?* If the only way to earn was to work as a prostitute, how could it be worse? I could disassociate, as I always had. I even had to do massages as the front for the place, but that wasn't often – we all knew what I was there for. Harry and Gretchen even took me out to get dresses as they had this notion that they were running some sort of high-class establishment. I don't do dresses – I never have – but I remember wearing a long, red expensive one with a stupid flower clip in my hair that they said was perfect. They also got me to agree to wear lots of make-up that one of the other girls applied for me. All of it had to be paid back to them though. Every 'cost' was a debt, everything they said I 'had' to buy meant that I was sinking deeper and deeper into being beholden to them.

We all had to use fake names as part of the aura of glamour too – all part of the notion that it was terribly civilised and consensual, as if you can really ever buy consent from a woman who is on the edge of her own life.

I remember it all much more clearly than I do the

other abuse, though. Every time, the client would ring the doorbell. Gretchen always answered the door – we girls weren't allowed. There was a front door, then a sort of cage screen thing, like a mosquito net, that we weren't allowed past – we could only come in the back way. The man would sit down and one by one each girl would come out, introduce herself, then go out the back again while he made his choice. It was like some sick audition process. *Pick me, pick me to fuck while I hate every fibre of your being, you disgusting excuse for a man!* The punter would say which girl he wanted and whoever he picked had to take him to a room with the menu.

The menus.

They really were menus, printed menus. They took the form of a list of what each girl would do and what it would cost. They listed each service and how much extra it was depending on what was requested. For example, it was $300 an hour for basic sex (about £100 back then). I remember it was $50 extra for anal or watersports, but I never did that – I count myself as lucky that I never had to do dirty play or bondage, but it was offered. I didn't do anything with shit but that was because no one asked for it – I would have had to do it if they had. I was never asked to do bondage either, but, again, I would have had no choice but to go through with it. There was always someone to do whatever a client wanted – there was nothing they could think of that Harry and Gretchen didn't have a girl for. I just did as I was told, desperate to get my visa and escape; I never said no.

Harry was scary, I would never have dared refuse him, but Gretchen wasn't mean at all. I can see now that between them they did a 'good cop, bad cop' routine and it worked well. If her softly-softly approach didn't work, he'd come in with the subtle threats. I saw him angry a few times and I would never have wanted to provoke that – plus he always had his 'driver' Doug to back him up, who was a very unpleasant man.

'This isn't what I wanted to do,' I once told Harry. 'I'd agreed to do reception, but I want to go home now.'

But he just laughed in my face and told me that with the amount of debt I had to repay, I wouldn't be going home for a long time.

I was getting in the same mess everywhere I went.

I had an address book that Harry took, and then he stopped me going out as he said it was a trap to get me deported. It was confusing as, at first, he said I was free to go, but when I started packing my stuff, he went crazy: he threw me into a door, hit me in the face and so I stayed. I didn't have the strength to fight that.

Even though the brothel was in the centre of the city and I might have been able to lose myself there, there was always someone guarding me. At the back door there was Frank and a Lebanese guy whose name I don't remember.

They treated me differently, I know that, because some of the others did get to come and go.

I was there for six months. At first, on reception, I got half of what I earned, then after I moved in, I got very little, as they had so many business costs and 'expenses' for me. Eventually, they started to dope me up with crystal meth to cope with the long hours they expected me to work. I was working 10am to 6pm, then going back at 8pm until 2am. On Fridays and Saturdays it was a 6am start, so after about a month of doing the job I was falling asleep, which made them give it to me to keep me awake. They said it would help to keep me awake and they were helping me so I just did as I was told (although again it was an 'expense' I had to pay for), but I hated it as it made me so paranoid. Then once I started. I took it every day, as I'm sure they knew would happen.

Every day I was strip-searched for cuts to make sure I wasn't self-harming again too. It was the first time that anyone had really noticed, and they hated the scars on my body. I hated that – they probably would have fined me if I had been harming myself and you could easily end up owing more than you earned.

The clients were professionals mostly as it was an expensive place. One guy came once a week; often he just lay next to me, he was nice. He used to want to fall asleep there and paid extra to do that. It was next to a casino so there was money, with lots of American sailors coming in when they were on shore leave. There was only ever one Asian guy and he was a complete bastard. You had to use protection in Harry's place but he refused to do so – I told them afterwards, but what could they do? He was also rough – it took me right back to when I was in England. He bit my lip and left a mark when I refused to kiss him; he was a horrible man.

There was one girl who worked at the brothel who terrified me. She was really scary, with dark spiked hair and a terrible attitude. I didn't like her at all, mostly because of my soft spot – animals. She had this little black-and-tan puppy and she was vile to it: she would punch him, hold him up by his collar and be generally cruel to him. One day I got into a big argument with her about it and Harry pulled me aside.

'Buy it off her,' he suggested to me. 'Buy the poor little bastard off her.'

'How?' I asked him. 'I've got no money.'

'I'll give you $100 of what you've earned,' he replied. 'It'll be nice for you to have that little fella to look after.'

Harry kept to his word. He gave me the money and I bought the pup off her. I really didn't think she'd go for it, but the money meant more to her than the dog. I know it was just adding to my debt but I didn't care. I had a puppy – I finally had a puppy. I used to wrap him up like a baby in a towel because it made him fall asleep, and I would fall asleep too whenever I got the chance, holding him in my arms. Between clients I used to just lay down on the bed with him. Whenever a client rang the bell, I'd gently lift the puppy and carry him out the back, put him down carefully (he always stayed asleep) and if I had to do the job then the other girls would look after him for me. When we were alone, he used to sleep under the covers with me.

I really loved him but the odd thing is, I never named him – I guess I always knew he would eventually go. In fact, I'd only had him for about two weeks before Harry said I had to get rid of him. I see it now as another means of control, though I was devastated at the time.

I'd been working there for a few months when Immigration somehow found out about me, and there were problems because I didn't have the right type of working visa. When I was called in, Harry came with me, and he didn't let me talk at all. The Immigration official kept trying to speak to me, but he talked over her.

She told him, 'It doesn't matter what you say, she's going home next week.'

Thank God, I thought. But all Harry did was phone a

friend of his, a politician, who wrote a letter and sorted it out, with the understanding that I would 'repay' him. Harry and Gretchen had good connections, I'll give them that.

Finally though, after another few weeks, I came to my senses and realised I'd had enough. This was no better than anything I'd been through before, no matter what lies I told myself.

There was a petrol station across the road from the brothel and somehow I managed to get out one day and rang Mum. I have to admit to you that she already knew what I was doing as I'd been allowed to phone her on previous occasions. I know that will make some people judge her. They will ask – probably not for the first time – why she wasn't being the sort of mum she should have been, the sort of mum a lost girl needed, but I just can't find it in me to be critical of her and I guess that's because I always hope one day she will be that person, she will be who I need her to be. If there's any chance of that happening, no matter how small, I want her to know that I always had hope, I always wished it would happen. She had even spoken to Harry before, and I think she was just glad I was away from where we lived and she didn't have to deal with my behaviour herself. I told her that things weren't too good and it would really help me if she could phone Harry or Gretchen and say she wanted me home for Christmas. To her credit, she did exactly that.

I suppose in an attempt to make his business seem less shady and to make it seem like I was in control, Harry agreed that I could go home if I promised to come back. Of course I had no intention of doing that, but acted as if I would love nothing better than to voluntarily return to the other side of the world and be a prostitute for a vile man who was conning me left, right and centre. He and Gretchen showed me what I'd been earning and said, 'You need to come back really as you have £30k of earnings.'

But I didn't care – I knew they would never give it to me.

They took me to the airport – to make sure I left, I guess – and I suspect Harry knew he would never see me again, because his last offer to me was that if I sent other girls out to him, he would pay me.

* * *

That Christmas, home again, I thought I must have had something tattooed on my forehead when I looked back at the past six months. Harry and Gretchen must have known I was like that – it must have been something I was doing. I still think that; I also believe it must be something obvious about me. It has to be – it can't just find you that many times, can it? It was only when I got home that I really thought back to how it had been in the brothel. When I was there, I was surviving, just getting through as I always did, but when I was back in England, I started to act out again. I got so drunk one weekend that I ended up in hospital twice with alcohol poisoning. My parents must have been fine with that (and everything else) because once I was home, it was like nothing had ever happened really. We didn't talk about Harry and Gretchen.

The confusing thing when I got home was that I missed Gretchen so much. I couldn't stop thinking about her. I remembered how she loved cartoons, and how she would sing to herself. She had piles of soft toys and she was always so giggly. I know it's crazy, I know she was just as bad as Harry, but I guess I was so desperate for a mother figure that I clung to anything. She used to say that she would like to adopt me – how twisted is that? She was complicit in the prostitution, yet I loved when she said anything that seemed vaguely caring, even though it was probably all an act. I'd managed to convince myself that Harry and Gretchen had treated me like family, the family I'd never really had, and I wondered how they were spending Christmas, with the tree they had let me decorate with baubles from the Disney store.

It was all so messed up; I see that now, but I certainly didn't back then. I had no idea just how damaged I was – and no idea that it could get even worse.

CHAPTER 10

'normal'

The first time it happened again was in the flat where I had been so many times before. Where I thought everything had been done to me. But I was wrong: there were more ways in which they could drag me down and degrade me.

There were two of them.

Ali. I knew him from before – I knew him from many previous occasions. Hassan's right-hand man.

But also a new man.

Zain.

Zain was very drunk. A good Muslim man, there to rape a 'white bitch'. I knew he wouldn't really be called

Zain – some of these men used their real names, but others found it so hilarious when they said what they were called that I knew it was all part of the game for them. The truth was, they could have handed me their passports and birth certificates and nothing would have touched them, so a fake name was just another great joke for these men.

They'd all been drinking so much that day and they'd been giving me vodka as well, as always – they'd get shitty with me if I didn't take it. They didn't like me saying 'no' to anything. They drank neat vodka too, nothing watered down for them.

I hadn't been back from Australia for long, only a matter of weeks, and I was still in a bit of a daze that I'd been dragged straight back into this. It had been the usual scenario. Walking down the street, one of them stopping in a taxi. 'Caitlin! Where have you been? We've missed you.' As if we were all great chums. As if they'd missed an equal, rather than a victim.

This particular afternoon we were sitting next to the bed in the room and things had changed a little. They had moved furniture into the room; it hadn't been there before. There was a table and two chairs next to the bed, I can see them now.

They sat there for a while, these two men, then Ali said, 'Come over to the bed with me.' It wasn't a request, it never was, but it looked as if Zain wanted to stay in the room while it happened, while Ali forced himself on me. Ali started taking my clothes off and I felt very uncomfortable – I don't know why as it had happened before with other men in the room, but there was just a feeling to it. Even though I'd just been used again in Australia, perhaps having experiences with kinder men had affected me without me realising?

I knew Zain was very drunk, so I tried to get up and leave. There was something about this that was making me feel very scared.

They started talking together, very quickly and in an extremely animated way. I couldn't understand a word as they weren't speaking in English but Zain was getting highly agitated. He pushed me back on the bed as Ali tried to calm him down, but it was all getting out of control really quickly. I managed to get out from under Zain's arm, but as I moved towards the bedroom door he threw a vodka bottle at me and went crazy. Ali just started pulling me back towards the bed. I tried to leave again but this time Zain had come behind me and I was sort of stuck between them.

I really don't want to say this, I really don't want to type it, but I think you've probably guessed. The shame I felt, but the pain more than anything, the pain was excruciating.

A pain in my heart and my head as well as my body. I felt ripped apart.

I have to say it, don't I? I have to write the words. Both of them violated me at the same time, and the agony I felt as Zain tore into me was unlike anything I had ever experienced. There was no warning. He was on me like a man possessed. I honestly don't believe anyone could have stopped him, he was determined to do this, determined to do the worst thing to me that I could possibly think of.

What goes through their minds?

They were both doing this to me at the same time while their friends were in a nearby room. Physically, they were so close to each other, but that didn't seem to matter: they still managed, they still found it sexually enjoyable. What sort of man does that? What sort of man even thinks of it?

This was my first experience of anal sex but it was by far the last. Afterwards I bled for days but I never went to the doctor. I was too scared and ashamed. I genuinely believed they had broken something in me and maybe they had. They said nothing while they were doing it, they were too busy concentrating, but afterwards? Afterwards it was as if it was the most natural thing in the world. They made me sit with them afterwards while they drank even more – a nice little party for them. After that they let me go. I didn't have to 'see' anyone else, so maybe they realised the magnitude of what they had just done. I walked almost three miles back home to my mum – I was only twenty but I felt a hundred years old. I don't remember if I cried, but I know I would've tried to get it together so my parents didn't see how much pain I was in.

A few days after the double rape, I was taken to another house by men I had never seen before, men who turned up in a taxi for me. *Was I being sold again?* I wondered. *Had the rape by Zain been a trial? Maybe they were testing me out to see how much they could do to me?* That was probably the scariest thought I'd had.

As I was walked through the door I had the same feeling of unease that I'd had with Zain and Ali. The door was locked behind me and about twelve men were sitting there. Ali was one of them, and it confirmed my fears about being sold on – he was the link, he was the connection.

He took me to a room through the back and apologised for what had happened the last time, but he was only saying sorry for his friend – he had just raped me, after all, but Zain had performed anal sex on me.

'Will you let me do to you what he did?' he asked. 'You've done it once, you can do it again and it'll be easier next time,' he told me.

'No, absolutely not,' I said, and he didn't that day, but it confused me why he was asking my permission, after all this time.

I was right: they had broken that taboo and now assumed that I was available for that too. That day I only had to see a few men, not all of them, thank God – I think they may have been testing me to see if they wanted to buy me.

* * *

The grooming never stops really and they always know who they will target next. Early on when they called me kafir girl, white bitch, white whore, I noticed they always put 'white' on it whenever they could. They swore at me the whole time, but I just got used to it – it washes over you as you're just this 'fucking white whore' after all.

This was how they spoke about all white women; it wasn't specific to me. Whenever they spoke of women, they used that language. They spoke of what they had done to other women – their own women – too. One boasted how he had sewn his wife up to make her tighter for him; he had done it himself. Maybe he said that on purpose to freak me out. He said it in English to his friend, probably so it had an effect on me. They certainly found it hilarious. I just blocked it out.

After that they just expected anal. In fact, I would say it became 90 per cent of my abuse. I think this was also partly because it had become so *normalised* in pornography, in society, with all the online porn sites and videos being shared like never before. It was as if it just wasn't a taboo anymore, so men – certainly men who bought women – just expected it. I think I was sold on again around this time, and I also think there was no going back: I'd been broken in and I could only see one alternative.

Back to Australia.

I couldn't face my family in Australia so I went back into the online chatrooms and started talking to people, telling them very little about me other than that I wanted to visit Australia and that I hoped to get away from some problems at home. I actually have no recollection of how I funded the cost of flights and the visa, but I do know that I met a couple called Don and Clare who said they would love to help by offering me a place to stay if I went over again. And they did. I might have been mad to trust anyone again, but I was desperate. The completely odd thing about them is that they were pretty normal. He made a few comments about the size of my chest, but he never did anything to me, and she was lovely.

I flew over just after Christmas and they collected me from the airport, saying that I could stay with them for the duration of my three-month visa if I liked.

They didn't seem to want anything from me, which was a complete novelty – I kept waiting for something, for it to turn sour, but it never did. I was never drawn into anything. They didn't even pry, they just seemed willing to offer a room to someone from the UK who they had met online – to me that actually made them the weirdos as I'd never come across anyone before who hadn't wanted to trade things for sex from me.

I don't know what I expected to happen in terms of my life changing while I was with Don and Clare, but nothing did. How could it? I didn't do anything. I tried to sleep as much as I could, and I tried to tell myself I was safe, but as the weeks went by on my visa, there was no miracle. No one came along to tell me how to live my life, or to offer me residency, and I was as depressed as I'd been at home – I didn't know what to do with freedom.

With only a few days left until I returned to England, I went out one night and got completely hammered. And met a man called Brandon. I'm actually not entirely sure what happened, though I remember feeling knocked off my feet after one particular shot he gave me so I'm not sure if it was spiked. I do remember that he was absolutely gorgeous, though, and very tall.

We went back to his place and the inevitable happened, but I was sort of zoning in and out by that time. He took me back to Don and Clare's the next day, and I never expected to see him again. A one-night stand for sure, but a one-night stand that hadn't left me feeling sore or in pain – I wasn't bleeding, I wasn't dealing with flashbacks. Just one man, just a one-off. Just...normal.

A couple of days later I flew back home.

The time in Australia hadn't made any difference – I'd wasted another opportunity – and the gangs in the UK got me very, very quickly. Within a matter of days I was back to it all again.

Nothing had changed.

Everything had changed.

Of course, I didn't notice for a while – I never did. My periods have never been right, I can never rely on them. But I was sick, *so* sick. I went to the GP because I thought I must have caught a bug in Australia. I'd been ill for quite a few weeks after I'd got back and there was lots in the news about SARS (a viral respiratory disease that can lead to pneumonia). My GP took a urine sample from me and it came back with the result I'd had before.

Positive.

Pregnant – again. I'd had three abortions by this time, however, this... this was different. I went to see a midwife and she said I was three months along. She also said the baby was due at Christmas.

Even I could do the maths on that one.

I knew the baby was Brandon's.

It had happened in Australia for sure and the first thing I thought was, *I can keep it. I can keep my baby.* Finally, I could have a child that was untainted by these men and all they did to me. I couldn't go through another abortion and, wonderfully, I wouldn't have to – this baby would make all the difference. *This baby would be mine.* I'd never have to see Brandon, I wouldn't even know how to contact him if I wanted to, so I could do it all alone and I relished the thought. At twenty-one, maybe this was the opportunity I needed. I'd been told 21st March was the conception date and I left on the 23rd, so there was no doubt. I was so relieved; not only was it not one of them but it was also someone I would never see again so I could just bring up my baby the way I wanted to.

I expected my parents to go crazy, as I said it had happened after a short relationship with a man in Australia – Mum wasn't too happy but Dad just said, 'Nice one.' *Nice one.* And it was. *It was nice – it was lovely.* When I decided that I would have the baby, I also hoped that it would finally let me escape: I would stay at home and have a normal life.

I was tiny for ages and I didn't tell anyone that I was pregnant as I had very little contact with people other than my abusers. I was still 'working' while I was pregnant but I think I stopped at about eight months – I just stopped getting calls and no one was turning up for me so someone must have passed the word round. It was clearly obvious by that time too.

It was the longest time I'd had away from them in this country. Before then, I'd felt like I was meant to be doing something all the time: now I was at home, I stayed in my room, I watched telly, and it was a luxury.

I didn't really feel a connection with the baby but there was still a lot of fear that they could turn up at any moment, so I thought that might have been part of the problem. I was still dead inside. I didn't sing or talk to my belly. *Once the baby gets here, I'll be OK though,* I thought.

Dad was really excited – he bought lots of clothes and just couldn't wait for his first grandchild. Every time he came home, he had something else. I went with him to get a pram and Mum was better towards the end, to give her credit. At the beginning, every time Dad brought another gift home, she'd just say, 'Oh for fuck's sake,' but that did pass in the last few weeks.

So I was left alone by the gangs, and I thought that was it. I didn't know how to look after a baby and I was scared but it was a million times better than the life I'd had.

I didn't know I was in labour at first – I got a bad tummy ache and thought I'd eaten too much at Christmas and had normal Boxing Day bloat! It got much worse though and by the time I got to hospital with Mum, I was 7cm dilated. We were taken into the delivery room and they were shocked I'd come in so late – it wasn't too bad but I guess, after everything I'd gone through, I had a high pain threshold. I don't remember much about my labour really – I think I must have dissociated as it was all happening in an area that had been the centre of my trauma. I don't know whether midwives take anything like that into consideration and I certainly didn't mention it, but it wasn't the first time I'd felt like I was being ripped in two.

Then, almost before I knew it, she was there.

My little girl: my Amy.

After only an hour and forty minutes, she came into the world, screaming and squalling, and desperately wanted: so, so wanted. I was scared of what sort of Mum I would be, but I knew I would do my best for her. She would be so loved, so pure – I would keep her from them, this perfect child, this untainted girl.

I didn't see her for a little while as they were cleaning her up, but I did feel happy, I know I did. I'd done it, this most normal of things, and maybe she could help me, maybe Amy would get me on the right path, away from them.

Away from that.

I lay there, letting myself hope a little, letting myself dream.

'Oh,' said the midwife from across the room. 'She has a blue spot on her back… Is her Dad Asian?'

Crash.

CHAPTER 11

repeat

The blue spot on her back was like a bruise. It was a sign of mixed race apparently.

'*No!*' I shouted. 'No – her dad's *white*!'

I looked at my mum and her face was like thunder. Silently, she stared at me and shook her head. Then I saw her, I saw the baby – I saw Amy. The midwife was holding her out towards me and I saw a tiny bundle with dark hair, curly, lots of it, brown eyes… and dark skin. She was beautiful, I could see that – but she was theirs. At that moment, I was just stunned.

They took me to a ward and I wasn't coping well at all. In fact, I was hysterical. I tried to keep my curtains closed for privacy, but the nurses kept opening them as they came and did their regular checks. Only two visitors were allowed at a time, unless it was for cultural reasons, then you could have as many as you liked. On this day, a Pakistani woman had given birth and there were so many men from her family on the ward. There was so much noise, and I was also having to deal with the fact that the obstetrician who had given me the episiotomy had been an Asian man too. I couldn't wait to get home, but I was also scared of how I would deal with this devastating news.

The reality kicked in for real when I was in my parents' house. I didn't breastfeed Amy, I just couldn't. I didn't want that element of touching, that proximity. At times I did hold her but I was completely thrown. I wasn't very good with her, I know – I did some of it but my parents did more. Dad did a lot: he would come for her when she cried and let me sleep, and he would take her for walks. I was starting to work out the dates – it must have happened very quickly, who had I been with in those first few days when I came back from Australia? I know that Ali had 'got' me but there had been others too. It could have been any of them.

I couldn't stop thinking about what had happened to me since that first phone call to Gordon, over 7 years before. I should have been loving my early days with a new baby, instead of having this whirlwind of terrible thoughts. Maybe it was partly my hormones, partly the shock of finding out Amy was one of theirs, but I was bogged down in a mire of it.

It's hard to escape these thoughts and these men; there was always one of them driving past when you know that many. I can list about a hundred men in detail, even with my poor memory, that I saw regularly just driving about looking for girls. When you see them every day, you can recognise them even from the back, but when they were new, I could tell that I hadn't seen them before. It's funny how your memory works. Sometimes it seems like the enemy.

How I wish I could forget all of it, but that would be too easy. I have holes in my memory but also bits that are razor-sharp. Those are the bits I'd like to rid myself – but, no, happy memories seem to disappear forever, while the detail of some abusers will be with me until the day I die.

What sticks with me is that they were so dirty.

Hardly any of them used protection – most people worry about that, don't they? They knew how many I'd been with, but they didn't care. Maybe they have specialised clinics as I never saw any of them at the ones I attended, and their wives must have been riddled with infection too.

Their wives.

I once saw one of the men with his wife – he brought over his entire family, including a baby in a car seat, to talk to me. It was all very general, 'How are you doing, how have you been?' It was so uncomfortable, but I guess that's what he got off on.

I wonder if she knew, I wonder if she blamed me?

You'll find this hard to believe but a couple of them would make me talk to their wives on the phone while they were raping me – I never knew what to say, they were raping me while they expected me to chat. One woman was friendly, she spoke some broken English, but who did she think I was? What did she think the grunts and groans were as she spoke to this strange young woman that her husband had passed the phone to? I found that utterly bizarre.

Such hatred for women.

There was one guy who brought his son to me for his sixteenth birthday – what a lovely gift, what a good father. 'This is my son, look after him,' he said to me, as he pushed the young man into the room, as if it was all terribly civilised. And he did it, the birthday boy did it. I had to 'see' the dad as well. I'd already met him a few times, but on that day, to celebrate, they both raped me.

So wrong.

Had he been told in advance? Had he been told he was a good boy and he'd get me as a present? Just like all the others, they never tried to justify themselves, they just did what they wanted.

What would I like to say to them now? Well, I'd rather not talk to them, but if I had to, I'd tell them how much hatred I have. I'd like to be a forgiving person, and maybe that will come with time, but it seems a very long way away.

I hate them – I hate them so much.

They have left me with this:

I don't like being touched.

I don't like anyone standing behind me, even those I trust.

I don't like crowds.

I don't like certain smells.

I don't like Bombay mix.

I don't like the stink of vodka – and it does smell, despite what people say.

I hate having to avoid certain areas.

I despise having to always look in taxis as they go past.

I'm on constant high alert if I'm just walking to the shop as I'm looking all over for things I could use for a weapon if I had to. I think of different scenarios the whole time.

I have dissociation often for no reason, even if I'm in Tesco. I'll have a trolley full of shopping and then it kicks in and I don't know what I'm doing anymore, so I leave the groceries in the middle of an aisle and go home, or just walk and walk and walk.

I forget how to do simple things.

If I think about what I'm doing, I can't do it.

I'm very forgetful – I can forget what I'm doing in the moment. I'll overrun a bath even while I'm watching it as my memory just goes.

I lose time, sometimes for hours on end – I just sit there doing nothing.

I can't stand to hear their music. That's one of the worst things – they always had it on, in the cars,in the house. It scares me.

I've overdosed a lot of times because of them.

I avoid lots of places: they will stop me thereand talk to me and ask me to find young girls. When I'm in the town area, I stick to the indoor shopping mall so they're less likely to see me.

I hardly ever leave the house as I worry about seeing them – it's not agoraphobia, just not wanting to see them.

I'm highly vigilant.

I always have my hoodie up.

I always worry that they'll get me.

I never really feel happy.

I yearn for sleep but I rarely get it – usually I have to knock myself out with pills to get it.

I feel sick talking to good people because I fear they will judge me.

I don't eat properly.

I have huge anxiety and panic attacks.

I have night terrors with shadows standing over me and they're still there for a while after I've woken up.

I need to have a huge dog in case they come to my door (but I love her, I really do love her).

I never have normal periods.

I have chest infections and lung problems all the time because of walking home in the cold and rain with hardly any clothes on. Every winter I get pleurisy because I have weakened lungs.

I can't have smear tests.

I can't bear anyone touching me down there.

I've never enjoyed sex.

I can't have blood taken because it triggers me.

I can't be hugged.

I have very little immunity from all of those times out in the cold wearing few clothes.

When a phone rings, I wonder if it's them, or I get a flashback to Gordon laughing at my mum and telling her I loved it and couldn't keep away.

I showered so often and scrubbed my skin so much between having to see men, I actually scrubbed skin off, and I still do that. I scrub my skin until it's scraped and really shiny and sore.

At times I still feel the need to shower several times a day when I remember things in detail or if one of them stops me and touches me at all, even it's just my arm.

I feel dirty all the time and need to scrub them off me even when I've had what has seemed a 'normal' day.

Is that enough, I'd say. *Haven't you done enough damage?* I think they'd laugh. I think they'd laugh and say, 'No, Caitlin. No, it isn't enough because you're still standing, you filthy white whore, and we won't rest while that's the case.'

Maybe they never think of me, maybe I'm the only one who remembers.

I used to lie there, with Amy in the cot beside me, with all these thoughts flooding through me. I was desperate to love her, desperate to be a good mum but I couldn't help thinking that because she was one of theirs, I would be dragged back into it, whereas if she hadn't been, maybe I would have had the strength to try and get out. And these awful thoughts wouldn't stop…

I had flashbacks of when I'd been living at the hostel and the boys there had been using me too. One boy raped me while three or four others stood and watched. It was on a table, outside my room in a hallway. My room was right at the end. The staff didn't really look out for us and I would never have screamed or shouted.

Afterwards he cried.

And *I* comforted him.

By then I was so used to it that I was the one who said it was fine and that I didn't mind.

Not really, not really.

A lot of the kids round the area knew what I was involved in because they saw me with all of these men. They were cruel, they taunted me and would shout that I should kill myself. At least they noticed – the adults seemed to be able to turn a blind eye to it all. I once got picked up near home, in a lay-by, and my mum walked past with the dog. She saw me getting into a car and said nothing, not a word. I often got seen there.

More flashbacks…

I was hit with a kitchen utensil, something with slots that hurt a lot, so hard it shattered. It was plastic, I had huge bruises from it. My legs, my back, my breasts... He loved that, that guy. They would just start doing it, very unexpectedly, the shock of it egging them on. After that he raped me and said, 'That's what you get for being with a strange man, you filthy white whore.'

One guy shoved a huge dildo in me, so big and hard that it ripped me, and that really did make me cry. I needed to go to hospital often but I never did. Once I was in a hotel with a guy who raped me anally and it was so rough I could see the blood pouring out as I crouched on all fours, and that lasted for days. I had a bad stomach for days afterwards, bleeding so much.

I was once taken to a flat above a shop, such a complicated set-up that I could never get away. I had to see a few men but more kept coming; they wouldn't let me leave but there were so many that I couldn't cope with any more and this time I did end up crying – I still had to see two more while I was crying. I was good at blocking things out but sometimes it broke through.

I remember one time being taking to a guy's house. There were three of them, and he took me into his daughter's room – now that was really fucked up.

He told me, 'You're better than my daughter at this,' and then he laughed. After that I just disappeared in my head – I remember coming out of it and he was done.

They all just laughed; they didn't use the word rape, but that's what it was – that's what it always was. Sometimes they seemed very angry but often they were just doing what they were doing: as far as they were concerned they were entitled to be that way.

All of this, all of this coming out while I lay there with my baby.

***

I couldn't see any way out but I knew I couldn't let my child be the victim of it too. I needed to get help.

I'd have to find a way to love her. I needed to concentrate on the fact that she was mine, not theirs. She only had a mother, she had no father. With just one parent, she might get through this. Maybe we both would – and it was certainly worth trying.

CHAPTER 12

help me

I've spent so long thinking no one can help me, but that's because no one has. I have told doctors, counsellors, psychiatrists, and many mental health professionals parts of my story. Highlights. Lowlights. I see the look in their eyes change, the alterations in body language, the way they take more notes or put their pen down. And I always interpret it as *you've gone too far, Caitlin.* Even when I've barely scratched the surface, I see these things and I think, *don't bother – they don't believe you.*

But I need help. I know I do. So, today, I'm going to try. Too many times, I agree to meeting a psychiatrist and ask for a woman, then, when I turn up, get told she's on call, or not turned up, and there's a man instead. It's always an Asian man. I'm finished before I start. To sit there and be expected to pour my life story out to a man who looks like all the men who did this to me – it's too much to ask.

But I'm going to try today.

I take a deep breath and pull my hoody a little closer to my aching body. I get this aching pelvic pain, a crushing feeling low down in me, which is just the same as when they press down on me with all their weight. It's there today, there as I walk in the doors of the mental health unit. So much they can't even see. Inside and outside.

It's a man.

Of course it is.

An Asian man.

Actually, I think I've seen this one before. I will try though, I really will. I know we have to go through the motions before we start, but I'll do that. I'm good at going through the motions.

'Hello, Caitlin – how are you today?'

It's always the same opener – how the hell am I meant

to respond? Say I'm great and then just leave? Say I'm awful and get straight into it? What do they want? I go for being evasive.

'Oh well, you know…sort of…I've been…well…' Sometimes, I think they don't really listen to the answer to that question anyway. I could tell them anything. I never would though; I have a list of what I'd never say because I've jumped through these hops before.

Don't say you're suicidal.

Don't say you self-harm.

Don't say you still want to kill Gordon.

Don't say you have overdosed so many more times than they know.

Don't say you're struggling to bond with your baby.

Don't say you want to go after every one of those evil bastards with a knife and stick it in them until they bleed and bleed and bleed and can never hurt another girl.

'How have you been?' he asks.

'Fine, thanks.'

He nods.

'Well, I've been looking over your notes – is there anything you'd like to talk about today?'

I knew I was on the clock. As soon as you're in there,

time is ticking. There isn't really the chance to waffle about, to avoid the difficult stuff…unless you want to, and, today, I didn't want to.

'Are you looking after yourself, Caitlin?' he continued. I knew the answer to this.

'Yes.'

'Are you having any thoughts of self-harm?'

Another easy one.

'No.'

Straightforward lies. The truth would be much harder.

'I seem to recall that you have had some trauma in your life?'

This needs to be danced around. Which one, doctor? Which trauma? I tilt my head a little and look quizzical. Let him come to me.

He checks my notes.

'An ex-boyfriend. Gordon?'

Ah. That's what we're calling him. An 'ex-boyfriend'?

'I wouldn't call him a boyfriend…' I say.

'No, no…an 'ex',' says the good doctor.

'Well, for him to be an 'ex', he would have had to be my boyfriend in the first place,' I point out.

A head tilt from him now.

'So – how would *you* describe him?'

Pimp.

Groomer.

Paedophile.

Bastard.

'It's complicated,' I agree, and he nods wisely.

I need to get this out, I really do.

'There is the carpet…' I start to say.

The way he keeps nodding really annoys me. He doesn't know about the carpet, no one knows about the carpet because I've never told anyone. If he wants to pretend he's heard this stuff, he's in for a shock, because once it's in your head, it never leaves.

'The carpet?' he asks.

'The same carpet – they seemed to have the same carpet everywhere, in all the flats, all the houses. I wonder why that was?'

And I'm off.

I know I have to tell someone, but I can't look the doctor in the eye. If I watch his face, I'm scared that I might see a change in it, or see those men when I look at him, so I keep my gaze on the floor. On the plain, beige carpet.

'It was red, dark red, with a navy pattern. Horrible. I stared at it so much. When I was lying down on the floor and they raped me, I'd put my head to the side and see the carpet. When I was on my knees and they were forcing themselves into me from behind? Stare at the carpet. When they left and I was waiting on the next one – stare at the carpet. I see that fucking carpet in my dreams and my nightmares.'

I pause, and he says, 'it sounds very…'

NO! I think. *Don't' speak – let me get this out.*

'There was one – I don't understand this. I can't work it out, but there was a man called Fayed. He was in his fifties, he would always get me in his car. The car was clean, I remember that – but I remember mostly that he always parked in places where people could see us. Car parks near to where dog walkers went, that sort of thing. Why did he do that? Did he want people to see? Was that part of it?'

I don't want an answer, not really.

'He wanted oral sex all the time. I worried about people seeing but he didn't. Disgusting, filthy.'

I'm not sure if I mean him or me.

'I must have dissociated I guess or I would have

gagged. I always would have gagged. Can you even imagine it, can you?'

If he wanted to hear this, I'd fucking tell him.

'Can you imagine being fifteen and a fifty-year-old man deciding he'd stuff himself in your mouth over and over again until he got what he wanted? Can you imagine that happening over and over again, so many men, so many men shoving themselves in, and you can't scream, you can't be sick, because they'd be so angry and they'd hit you and they'd slap you and your jaw would crack and your lip would swell and your ribs would ache...so, you just zone out. This dirty old man calls you a white whore with every thrust, and you have to take it, you have to.'

I stop.

Catch my breath.

Try not to go back there.

'But that's not what I don't understand. He wanted that, and he felt he was entitled to that – and maybe he was because people must have seen us, it was daylight, and they walked past, and maybe they thought I was a filthy white slut too. I wish I knew what they were thinking – or maybe I don't. Maybe I don't.'

'Do you want to hear more?'

I don't wait for him to answer.

'There was another group of guys on a separate occasion. I had to give head to them all around the side of a building, then they took me off to the local country park. All of them raped me by the lake there – all of them. Afterwards, one of them gave me £10 and said not to tell his girlfriend. That was thoughtful, wasn't it?'

I'm still not looking at him, still not judging his reactions and I can't allow myself to think about whether he is judging me. I try to guess what he would ask me if he didn't have to only talk in psychiatrist-speak. If he was actually allowed to ever ask me something, I bet he'd want to know why I didn't leave, why I just didn't' stay away.

'I couldn't get away you know – I couldn't just say "no, thanks, no rape for me today!" because they had groomed me so perfectly. From the start, from Gordon, I was so ashamed. There were photos and there things I knew would get me into trouble, like using Mum's bedroom to get raped in. That was bad of me, of *me*. And then it was compounded every single time they got me. They were ashamed of nothing, but I was ashamed of everything. In my mind, they ruined me so completely from the start that there was no going back. There *is* no going back. I can't refuse them, because they have turned me into something that is so horrible, I can barely stand to even look at myself.'

I had to be careful here, not talk of the things I did to myself, not talk of how I wanted to stop it all permanently at times. I take a moment, and I do something silly – I look at him. He's writing, and I think that's bad. I must take too long to get back to it, because he, eventually, looks up and says, 'how are you?'

It breaks the spell. It breaks the spell of me trying to tell someone.

'Fine thanks!' I giggle.

Later, I ask for copies of my records to see what the psychiatrist has written, to see whether there are any answers.

They say:

Caitlin is currently working as an escort.

Thanks, I think. *Thanks.*

***

It wasn't the first time I'd seen some medical records – there were others that gave me a glimpse of me as the professionals saw me, but they never really solved the puzzle. Why me, and why did no one ever do anything?

It was all so stark on the page but I knew the human story behind it, the story of me:

History of self-harm.

Very quiet.

Flat mood.

Unable to disclose problems.

Vunrable female (sic)

Ask me more then, ask me why I am so 'vunrable'.

Doesn't like crowds.

Slight anxiety.

Hot and sweaty.

Really? 'Slight'? I'm hot and sweaty because I'm terrified of you, I'm terrified of everything. I never feel safe, I'm always watching, always waiting for someone to grab me. Yes, slight anxiety from that – well spotted.

Sometimes though, there would be a report that seemed to understand.

'Caitlin is presently complaining of low confidence

and being nervous of going out and blaming herself for previous life events,' wrote Dr M in December 2000. 'Considering her history of being physically abused and pushed into prostitution, this is hardly surprising.'

That sort of understanding, even though it was still pretty superficial, was so much more than I usually got. The doctor who dismissed me as an 'escort' also said, 'Caitlin was well-dressed and made good eye contact. There were no psychosis or mania or hypomania. There was no evidence of major depression. There were no active suicidal or homicidal thoughts.'

He was Pakistani.

Another doctor who was also Pakistani, writes: 'Psychiatric problem? Investigation – no further investigation needed. Treatment – no further treatment given. Additional treatment – verbal advice given. Disposal – discharged.' As if it was all sorted.

Another Pakistani doctor – 'She continues to put herself in vulnerable positions.' My fault, then, my fault.

Another one – 'She knows she is fully responsible for her actions.' I did, actually – most of the time, I blamed myself.

I wondered what they thought of me, all these men who listened to me, telling them what those men had done to me. Did they think I was just a rambling racist? Did they take it personally? I tried so hard so many times, but there just seemed to be a block. If I was coherent enough to tell them, I wasn't bad enough to need help. If I was a mess, they would never believe me as it was all so unbelievable anyway.

CHAPTER 13

my world

I should have been wrapped up in the cocoon of my first baby – instead, I was battling demons every moment of every day, internally and externally.

I still wasn't bonding well with Amy, but Mum was also telling me I didn't care for her and everything I was doing was wrong. And I believed her: I did the practical things OK but not the bonding..

I can't remember the first time it happened again after the birth, as it all seems a blur of the same thing. They certainly never once mentioned that I'd been away. It was just back to it. Mum and Dad looked after

Amy when they turned up at the house to collect me, but as usual a blind eye was turned to that. I was so numb, so heavy with the horror of it, that I don't think I questioned why my parents never stepped in. I was a mother now and I wanted to protect my daughter – why didn't they have that same attitude to me? I was so young, and I'd just given birth, but they seemed unconcerned when the streams of Pakistani men started calling for me again – the taxis, the doorbell ringing at all hours. I'd just hand Amy over and say, 'Can you watch her, please?' and then I'd go.

It was almost inevitable that I got pregnant again very quickly. I was four months along, just like the last time, when I found out and Amy was turning over by then so, working it back, I think they got me when she was three months old. Mum was furious. It was the sickness that alerted me, just as before. I went to the GP and the test was negative for some reason, so I went back as the vomiting wouldn't stop. This time I asked for a termination, but it was too late.

'You're under twelve weeks but not by much,' the doctor told me. 'You'll have to go to a BPAS [British Pregnancy Advisory Service] clinic as you're too far gone for me to help.' When I got there, they did a scan and there was another shock waiting for me.

'You're at least sixteen weeks,' said the woman scanning me.

When I asked if I could get a termination done that day, I was told that it would take up to a fortnight to get the appointment. I think I must have been about nineteen weeks when they finally arranged to do it.

I turned up with Mum and Dad on the day – she was going to go in with me, but Dad said that he would wait outside. Just before we left the car, I had a panic attack.

'I can't do this,' I told them. 'I can't.'

Looking at Amy in the car seat, I just felt that I couldn't kill another child.

'Well, you've no choice,' said Mum. 'There is no way you can have another baby as a single mother. What on earth would people say?'

I looked to Dad.

'She can do what she likes,' he told her. 'We'd cope.'

'No, absolutely not. I'm not having it,' Mum insisted.

'Please,' I begged her, 'please don't make me do this. I don't want to do it, let me go home.'

'Well, you should have thought of this a long time ago,' she said coldly. 'Get a move on, they're waiting.'

Mum stayed in the waiting room while I went for the scan. I was crying the whole time. When the obstetrician looked at the baby, she said, 'Oh, he's kicking me!' That was the worst thing – I knew that I was far along, but I didn't expect her to say something like that. 'I'll have to check they'll still do it,' she told me. 'You're much further than I expected.'

But they did. It was under general anaesthetic, and when I came round to leave, I just wanted Mum to gather me up in her arms. But she seemed so cold and distant. She never once hugged me, she just seemed so angry and annoyed that I'd wanted to change my mind. After eating some soggy toast I was sent home and the whole journey back I felt crampy and groggy. I was bleeding heavily and very drowsy. Also, I was extremely low – I hadn't wanted this. Afterwards there was no counselling offered, that was it.

Back home I went straight up to my room, with Amy's cot in there, bleeding heavily and feeling completely empty. Mum had made me get rid of all Amy's stuff that she had grown out of when she knew

I was pregnant – I guess to emphasise that keeping the baby wasn't an option. I can't remember much more around that time, just sadness.

* * *

Over the next three years, my life didn't change: this was my world, a world of hell and pain and loneliness. During this time I had many suicide attempts, one soon after the abortion my mum made me have. I looked up methods to do it successfully, desperately hoping it would work this time – there are websites that help. I took a little extra than was suggested to make sure but I still survived. How my mental state at the time affected Amy's early life, I can only being to imagine, especially as I was a single mother.

More men came all the time – they brought a friend, then they brought another friend, or a cousin, or a business partner, all for me to 'take care of'. There could be eight or ten in a room at a time quite easily. They called it a 'party' when they had more than one girl and a lot of men, especially when they got girls from the children's home (which they always did), and they had friends coming over from abroad – 'Look after him well, leave him happy!' they'd say.

The only time I ever got in trouble was if I argued about what they wanted. I hated anal, I hated all of it, but that and bondage especially made me retch. To me it felt dangerous – they might not stop, they might not know when to stop. There was often a holdall in the room with stuff that they could use if they wanted, whips and cuffs. I remember one of them really liked all of that and he would lay it all out on a dressing table and I didn't even know what half of it was. He liked to take his time selecting what to use on me. The ones who liked bondage were dressed more like businessmen, I would say. They came on their own, and they left immediately afterwards.

With anal you never knew when it would happen, but it was becoming more and more common. I saw that change – they all wanted it, they all loved it. They never seemed bothered about getting caught – I don't think they thought they were doing anything wrong. More and more taxis were turning up, more in London cabs too as time went on.

By now I was starting to know the signs of being

pregnant and I was catching it earlier so I could get the morning-after pill at the hospital. I found ways to avoid Mum knowing too. I'd get her or Dad to watch Amy, saying I was going shopping – and there were times when it would be in and out on the same day, and they would have no idea.

This had become my normality. It wasn't touching me but that only seems bad now. I was glad of feeling nothing then. Now, I feel guilty: I shouldn't have done it, I should have had my children and protected them. I tried the pill too but I'd developed an eating disorder, so I was vomiting the tablets up. I saw different GPs too so they never joined the dots – I knew the procedure, I knew what would happen.

I dissociated.

I had to perform oral sex on so many men who would always made me swallow afterwards and I was sick – I think that added to and explained my eating disorder as this was something I could control when I threw up rather than it being something they had forced down me.

A couple of them wanted to take me to Pakistan. They wanted to take me to the 'home country' as they called it – they would say it afterwards; maybe they rewrote what had just happened and decided we could live happily ever after. It seems like they could rewrite most things. Hassan once said that he wanted me to marry some men to get them in the country. He told me it would be worth £10k, but I wouldn't get any of that, would I? They said all I'd have to do would be just to have some of his clothes at my house as well as his toothbrush, know his favourite colour for Immigration, then divorce after two years. Hassan and Ali both suggested it actually – it just never happened.

Around this time, I would have been twenty-four or so now, other people came along and they made it clear they were in charge. All of a sudden there was a guy called Robin. I was seeing the Pakistani men too, but Robin must have bought me because he was by far my busiest source of 'work'. I can't even remember the first time I worked for Robin; always I just did as I was told. He would say, 'I have a friend, or I know a guy…' But I knew the dynamics were changing.

He put me on the website *Adultwork*. To start with, I certainly didn't know about *Adultwork*, but I soon learned. Sites like that were just starting to become really popular and it was easy for him to put me in a hotel for a whole day with one man after another who had booked me for whatever they wanted. All the while my parents looked after Amy. They just knew I had a job, but they never asked any questions.

I was between two bosses then – the Pakistanis and Robin – and it was hard to please them all. I was taken to a lot of hotels, sometimes ordinary chains, but also some nice hotels in London – it was always a hotel with Robin, never a flat or house. The enquiries came to Robin through the website and he knew what I would be doing, but I never did – he had his little notebook with times and requests but I never saw that. He sat outside in his car to make sure he was keeping to the schedule, what time I would need to finish for the next one, and he would always text me. The phone would go and I'd know I had to get the client to go.

I had no idea how Robin and the Pakistani gang worked together; did he work for them, did he give them a share of what he made from me? I do remember when I first met him, as he was brought in to film a video with me – was that when the deal was done?

He was nicer than them, I guess. By then I had such a physical reaction against Pakistani men that I was almost relieved when it was someone white – they still did awful things but they weren't as rough, most of them. Better rapists, I guess. They were more human if that makes any kind of sick sense. Robin did say to me, 'These guys treat you like shit, I'll treat you much better,' but I knew he was scared of them too as he never said that in front of them or in a way they could hear – he was always polite to them.

Robin told me that he would pay me. And he did – he would give me more than the others ever had. After one day in a posh London hotel he gave me £700, but I have no idea how much he had made. I was probably seeing four clients a day, so it had dropped down a bit, but some of the hotel clients took a while as they would buy me for more than an hour at a time depending on what they wanted. When we drove to other places, other hotels around the country, Robin talked to me, often about his girlfriend – that she was nice and into this stuff as well. I suppose he was making out that I was choosing it, that this was what I liked sexually.

Most of Robin's clients were white, but some of them were Asian although they seemed different – they were pretty much all businessmen. I just thought all men were like that and sometimes I still do – I think most men who pay for it know the full story really, don't they? Often they pretend it's the woman's choice, but that's just a lie they tell themselves. *In those houses, how could they have thought I was choosing that?*

These men using the website must have been family guys who saw me in their lunchtime then went back home at night. I felt so guilty for their families but why did they need to do that? They can't do to their wives what they want to do to me maybe. They obviously don't care though, do they?

***

With the gangs, they liked it rough whenever and however, but with the website, I was told exactly what the client wanted – anal or video or unprotected, they would book me for something in particular. I knew what I'd be doing. Pornography became so accessible and it was normalised – but it *isn't* normal. You don't do that if you care for someone – it's dehumanising, it's about the man getting what he wants. There's no connection, he doesn't even have to look at the woman's face. I had one guy, when I told him he was hurting me, which I had built up the courage to do with Robin's clients, he said, 'Do you think I care? I paid for this.' I think a lot of them wanted to hurt me and some wanted to degrade me; they wanted me to be doing something I didn't want to do.

They all had phones and easy access to the internet – if they filmed me, it could be out there in seconds. Technology had changed so much and I started to find myself online. There were some Kosovans who met me through the Pakistani gang, three of them, only once – they filmed me on their phones. Some said it was for their own personal use, but I hate to think where all of those videos are. I know now that these men sometimes need new film to join groups – there is definitely one film on *Adultwork* to this day, however hard I try to get it taken down. They present these women as legitimate, bored housewives – consensual, adults being adults – but they can pretend what they like, this is what most of the women and girls are going through.

Once *Adultwork* took off, that changed everything – it allowed so many to say that what they wanted was the norm. I've even been reviewed online, how dehumanising is that? They're describing rape, they're *reviewing* rape. Then they complain that a girl doesn't look like she's enjoying it – why the hell do they think that is then?

By this time everything in terms of sex seemed that it was just becoming more acceptable – they asked for watersports a lot, them doing it to me. That isn't sex, is it? There was a sheet of paper Robin gave me, from his notepad, with the times and what they wanted – like *John, anal, 1pm, 40 minutes.* Sometimes I was barely given ten minutes in between depending on the time they picked. They gave me the money, I took it down to him, then I went back to the room. The hotel staff must have seen me. My head was full of it – I had to keep so many people happy.

Except for me – always except for me.

CHAPTER 14

Stop!

Stephen was a client I met through *Adultwork* who wanted anal straight away. I used to be booked in for him in a cheap, shitty hotel. If I had a lot of men in one day, I got a better hotel, but if it was just one on his own, then the standard would drop. I saw him at least once a week, and he travelled quite a distance to see me.

By now the Pakistani gangs were less in the picture. I must have made them all a fortune over the years, so I wonder now if Robin paid more for me to be able to get me on an almost exclusive deal? It's weird how people seemed to disappear over time.

Stephen had a plan to make me pregnant – he said he wanted that from the start. He asked Robin if he could, if that would be alright with my owner not me, and Robin told me to just pretend – he used to make the others use protection.

Stephen was always saying how he liked the bump on mums-to-be; he didn't want involvement with any baby, he just got off on pregnant women – like a lot of men do, I guess, or there wouldn't be such a market for pregnancy pornography. He wanted to have a pregnant woman to buy sex with for nine months, from start to finish.

He once said, 'If you didn't have a kid, I would want a relationship with you,' as if he was doing me a favour.

Why would I want a man like that in my life? A man who thinks like that?

Every month Stephen would ask if I was pregnant – I saw him a lot. He would do anal then he would try and make me pregnant. I think he just did normal sex to try and make me conceive, he didn't actually want it that way. I did try and always catch it; I tried the morning after pill as well as being on the pill, but nothing was ever reliable with me as I was sick so much from self-harm, my eating disorder and anxiety.

And I could never get injectable contraception as my terror of doctors and needles was so bad, even worse since I'd had Amy, so the inevitable happened.

I was twelve weeks before I found out.

This time I was sick much less actually – in fact, probably less than when I wasn't pregnant, and it started later. I didn't tell Stephen, but I did tell Robin. He was furious; I expected him to hit me, but he didn't – he just said I was stupid and thought I'd lied about taking the morning-after pill.

Stephen eventually noticed. I didn't want to tell him, I certainly didn't want him to think I'd done it for him, but once he realised, he wanted to see me all the time. It was pretty disgusting, seeing how much he enjoyed it. His hands were all over my belly – he rested his head on it, he was obsessed.

I didn't want another abortion, I knew that: I would have had to go to BPAS again and I couldn't bear it. That would have been harder than having a baby. I still felt so guilty, so horrible about the late one.

I guess Robin must have put me on *Adultwork* as a pregnant option as some perverts loved that and I got a lot of business.

Dad was fine about my pregnancy, but Mum was not happy at all – I got shit off her about how stupid I was, but there was no way I was going to have an abortion. I did 'work' throughout the pregnancy but I pretty much knew that Stephen was the father of this baby, considering the men I saw through Robin wore condoms. There would be no surprise like there had been with Amy.

Ruby's birth wasn't easy as the placenta attached to my muscle; they found that out afterwards and tried to pull it out as it was stuck. It was an Asian doctor again and I had flashbacks the whole time. His whole arm was up there and I got in such a state that I told him to get the fuck off me. I was freaking out and I just didn't want him to touch me.

The doctors said I would die, but I didn't care, so after forty-five minutes they knocked me out.

When I came round, it was just me and Ruby for a while. As soon as I saw her, there was a massive relief. She was tiny, only 5lb, and immediately I felt protective of her. She was blonde, although there wasn't much hair; she was just so small and vulnerable.

From the start she looked like him – she looked like

Stephen, but I didn't care. I was just so relieved that she wasn't from one of the Pakistanis, a product of such abuse, that I could deal with the fact that her father had bought me too.

I loved her immediately. I couldn't deny that it felt different – I love both my children now but it had to grow with Amy.

***

Amy was four years old when Ruby was born and she absolutely loved her. Just before the birth, I'd managed to get a small council house of my own so I took Ruby in with me for a while then the girls shared a room when she was old enough.

She was such a good baby – she was like a little doll and none of her clothes fitted. Dad went out and bought premature stuff but all that was too big as well. She was perfectly healthy though. My overriding feeling was that it all felt more normal and I think that was purely because she wasn't Asian.

I was allowed a bit of time off too, more than with Amy, because Robin was in charge now. He was friendly and texted me a lot, and it was nearing Ruby's first birthday by the time I went back. Although he asked me if I was ready, he didn't push me. And I was grateful – how mad is that? I was grateful my pimp was being nice to me and allowing me a bit of time before he sold my body again to make money for him.

What a nice man.

I never heard from Stephen again once I'd had Ruby: it wasn't a baby he wanted, it was the use of a pregnant woman's body. The Pakistanis had faded out for a while and Robin was definitely in charge of me. I didn't want to piss him off though, I never want to piss anyone off, so that's probably why I was so pathetically grateful that he wasn't pushing. I didn't know in advance that he would leave me alone for a year, so every day I wondered if I would have to go back that day. And I wondered when the Pakistani men would start again – I still worry that they will drag me in again, I worry all the time.

But one thing I knew, I wouldn't be left alone by these men forever. At least they didn't know where I lived now – though I could never really be sure that Robin wouldn't just tell them my new address. I had two babies to look after now, rather than one, but I knew it made no difference to them. In fact, I had two miscarriages after Amy, when some of Robin's clients refused to use contraception, but I never went to the clinic, I never raised any alarm. In my heart, I knew I'd never have another baby – there was no way my body could do it again.

When Ruby was about three years old, I was walking her in her pram with Amy trotting alongside when a man stopped to speak to me. He chatted as if I was an old friend he'd just caught up with; he said everyone missed me and hoped they would see me soon.

Sick bastards.

It just never changed. These men had been around for more than ten years. They were still untouched, they were still doing it. Over the years there must have been so many like me, but there are too many of them. There will always be a supply of lost girls and I feel there may always be a refusal on the part of those in power to deal with their abusers.

I felt used, worn out, like I'd been old for years but at the same time, I felt fourteen again as soon as they spoke to me. I feel like I have to do as I'm told, like I'm stuck there. They started to ask me for younger girls but it didn't stop them from going for me too – I wish it had, I wish getting older had put them off.

***

Over the past few years my memory hasn't got any better. Even writing this book has been a struggle because I jump from one thing to another, I go between memories like a cat jumping on hot tiles. I think I can settle on one thing, then another part of it flares up and I run from the memory, only to find another one waiting. It's as if I'm in a room of boxes, each one holding something worse than the last, each one waiting to spring open and throw something hideous at me. I don't want to open them, I want them to stay closed forever, but what if there are good memories in there too? The fear is that room will keep getting more boxes added to it – more bad things, more awful stuff that will spring out when I least expect it.

I can remember the last time they got me though.

I was raped in my living room. It was a weekend, I know, as the girls, who were now nine and five, were with my parents. It was night-time and a man knocked on my door – he must have followed me home. He asked me for a younger girl, I said I didn't know any, so he put his foot in the door then pushed in and raped me. Afterwards he said, 'Really nice to see you. I've really missed you, there's been no other girl like you. We've all been looking for you – you're so different to the other girls, you were never any bother.'

Then he left after telling me that I was one of the better-behaved ones.

I showered straight away. He didn't use protection so I tried to get as much of him out of me as possible. I took codeine – a lot of codeine. I was so disappointed when I first woke up – so pissed off to still be here. Now I remember: it was a school holiday and the girls were away for a week with my parents. My head was in a bad place anyway. I had researched my suicide online but it still didn't work; I just had real trouble waking up for four days. I must have a body of steel. So I phoned NHS Direct and spoke to a nurse as I was throwing up blood. She wanted me to get checked out but I thought they'd lock me up. I said I'd taken too many tablets and she was shocked when she heard how much. I could barely get up – I woke up a few times, got myself some water but my legs were like jelly. It was a struggle and most of the time I was asleep.

But Amy and Ruby – they were always there in my mind, making me think that I could never really leave. So, I put the new attack in a box, and I stamped down the lid and hoped against hope that it would stay the fuck in there. But it won't – I know it won't.

And there's always more to add.

I think the guy who raped me in my own home must have spread the word. What would he have said? *'I've found Caitlin and guess what? She's still a stupid white bitch – she still lets you do anything you want to her. So go ahead, boys, go ahead!'*. A couple of months later, when my girls were with me in the house, two taxi drivers knocked at my door, one called Mo, a really nasty bastard who'd been around for years. They had knocked on my door together and like a fool, I answered. Mo didn't rape me but his friend did, and it seemed like I would never escape. I even remember one of my neighbours seeing them leave and saying, 'Why don't you ever leave this poor girl alone?'

I was distraught, knowing that these men didn't care

that my daughters were both in the house. It brought everything back up to the surface.

I dropped the girls with my parents, and that night I tried to kill myself again and was taken to hospital.

Another overdose – a big one. Jack Daniel's, wine, tablets… I rang 999 for help as I'd woken up and was terrified. My biggest fear is spiders and I was hallucinating them everywhere. I insisted it was an accident but they knew it wasn't; they always do. An ambulance came but I couldn't walk by that time and they had to carry me. The guy said, 'Don't ever do that again – this is horrible stuff and you will bleed from every hole in your body.'

The next thing I recall is being on the emergency room bed, in and out of consciousness and my speech was slurred. I had a drip in me which I hated because of the needles and it was making me panic. When I tried to get up, I collapsed – I couldn't walk. The next thing I knew, I was waking up on the cardiac ward attached to a machine. I asked to go home but they said they were struggling to get my heart rate up, it was going under 50, but I needed out of there. My notes say, very plainly: 'The patient has chosen to go home against medical advice'.

I had to face the fact that I'd been raped while Amy lay in her cot in the next room. They'd come for me while my children had been there – and it was that, that and the fact they were looking at my babies in a way that terrified me, which made me act.

***

I needed to get away, I knew that – and I needed to take the girls with me. I was in a frenzy and immediately made plans to go to Australia and stay with another cousin, Freya, who lived far away from Mary and Melbourne and all of my past there.

I decided that I had to tell her everything – and I hoped to a God I didn't believe in that someone would finally help me. To my sheer relief, after all this time, Freya believed me and said she'd help me try and get some sort of safety visa if I went over, if we could only persuade the authorities that my girls were in danger if we all stayed in the UK. She asked me to make a list of what had gone on – but where would I start? The guy who said he was HIV+ and always wanted unprotected sex? Was that a lie to keep me in place? The ones who spat on me while they raped me? Those who bit my breasts and pissed on me? The man who wanted to strangle me and made me think I was going to die? Then there was the one who throttled me so hard that I had bruises for months. What about the ones who liked to pour hot wax from candles on me as part of their bondage fantasies? What about the whips and chains and handcuffs? The kicking and slapping and punching too? And the ones who ignored me when I said it hurt? Those who laughed and said, 'Why would that matter?' – the fathers, the sons, the grandfathers, the upstanding citizens... How could I ever find it in me to tell everyone everything?

I thought of all the times I went to places when it was dark. Sometimes they would say, 'Just go to the house where the door will be open.' There would be a door partially ajar, always with all the lights off. I'd be shitting myself – but what could happen that was worse than my everyday life anyway? So I'd go in and they'd shut the door, they'd grab me and walk me up the stairs, that happened a lot. Where were the women in those homes? They used each other's houses when they were empty, I think, but I'm just assuming that. I remember there was a women at one flat they always used, she was banging at the door and screaming in her language. She must have known her husband was in there – what was her life? I just thought they must be having awful existences too, but I didn't want to think about the fact that these men were fathers.

If they did this to me, what was to stop them abusing their own kids? Who would stop them?

CHAPTER 15

lost

There have been so many that I don't know the dates or details, so let me tell you about my lost babies.

All my lost babies.

At this I struggle. How can that be right? How can I forget how many lost souls there were?

I think I've worked it out. There were eleven pregnancies. Eleven… That's a lot, isn't it?

Let me remember you, let me recognise you for once in your little existences.

There was the abortion Gordon arranged.

(I'm scared. I'm so scared. Why does no one ask my name?

Why is no one talking to me? Please make this stop – I can't have a baby, I know that, but I don't want to do this, I don't want to do this.)

Then I had one more. The same again – the same sickness, the same not really noticing until I couldn't ignore it any longer.

(No, no! This can't be happening. I need to deal with it, don't I? I need to go through it again. And I will – I'll deal with it because I can't have them, I can't bring a child into this.)

Then my daughter, my first girl. With the hopes I had, the hopes that she wasn't theirs, that she was all me and that random man in Australia. That white man and, yes, that did matter. My baby. Tainted by them, and me – tainted by me too, because what a mother I am! What genes to have... What blood to have rushing through your veins. A rapist father – God knows which one – and a white whore mother. Will you survive it, Amy? *Will you?*

Then one more.

Then one more.

Then one more.

Then one more.

Four more little lives, all snuffed out. One of them I wanted. And I did – I really wanted that one. But Mum said no and Dad said yes – Mum won.

Then Ruby.

Ruby with her white father. Still a man who bought me, still a man who thought that was fine, but his whiteness matters. I bonded with her, I did. I feel love for both my children but this one was easier. So, more guilt – guilt for Amy. Guilt that it wasn't so easy to love her.

Then one more.

Then one more.

But this time miscarriages, threats of ectopic pregnancy. Doctors saying I need tests to make sure. Me, panicking – no tests, no intervention, no prodding at my body and holding me down. Not again. They said I might die, I told them I didn't care.

So … eleven.

Eleven pregnancies – two babies out of all that.

I don't remember who the fathers were – well, I don't know, do I? I couldn't tell, there were so many of them. So I made the decision not to have those babies – I did, I decided. It was me although the first one after Amy was my mum's choice really. I went to a proper abortion clinic but it was no better; I remember begging my mum to keep it.

'Absolutely not,' she said. 'You're already a single mum, what will the neighbours say?'

That's right, Mum, it's the neighbours who matter – they're the important ones.

She made sure I went through with it.

Dad said, 'Fuck her, you don't have to do it,' but he dropped us off and left.

Why did you leave, Dad? Why didn't you help me keep my baby?

They told me how they would do it – they have to tell you so you know.. I didn't want to know but it was part of my punishment, I deserved it.

Some were tablets, some were more invasive – how can that all be a blur to me, how can I not know which one is which? I've closed myself off, I know that, but those babies couldn't have been born into that horror. After a while I didn't care that much – I was so used to it, I was numb. That's what they'd made me. People who are pro-life will hate me anyway, but what can I say? What horror must I have been going through to make me numb to that? Knowing where those babies had come from wasn't easy, what a thing to start your life with. I wouldn't want lots of kids I had issues with. The struggle to love Amy didn't last too long but it was there to start with. Actually, I'm not sure it really was a struggle to love her, more a struggle to accept where she was from. I just see her as my own now, there is no father. Same with the second, they are just my babies.

But I know it's one of them, and I'd be so worried that they would find out and they would get the kid. And I was terrified they would be girls – they wouldn't have hesitated to take them or abuse them, I think. I was so fucked up but I dissociated. Now I think, *what about all of those lives, all those babies I got rid of? Is Hell waiting for me? Is there worse than I've already been through?*

I'm not spiritual but I wish I could say to my children, *I did it for you, I knew what life you would be brought into. No matter how numb I was, I always put you first.*

I've probably not told you the half of it. So, are you surprised? Would you even admit to all this? I wonder if my children are all together, watching me. Would they wish they'd been born, no matter what? But I can't go down that road – I couldn't then and I can't now. How could I have brought more children into this world? I'm surprised I even managed two, given the legacy of the abuse on my body.

It's done.

It's done now.

Maybe I'm damned, but I have to believe this – I have to believe I did it for them.

CHAPTER 16

listen

It took a couple of months to arrange everything with Freya and I arrived in Australia with the girls in December 2013. I hoped we'd never leave.

One of the groups that helped me was called ACRATH (Australian Catholic Religious Against Trafficking in Humans) and they were extremely supportive. I have to be honest – I'm not a religious person, but I was desperate. I would take help from anyone, from anywhere, and I could now see that there were some good people within religious groups; they weren't all like the religious types who had been so active in my abuse over the years.

I'd been warned that I would have to buy a return, as before, or I wouldn't get in, but as soon as I arrived, Freya helped me apply for protection. I was also warned that it would be hard as it would open the floodgates and that, because I was white, it could cause political problems as it would imply that the British police and government couldn't protect their own people.

Freya wrote a wonderful application for me, but it was hard to see it all in black and white like that.

She said:

> 'Amy is a nine-year-old English girl. She is very gentle-hearted, loves all the pretty things and adores her animals. She is also completely unaware of the fact that a large gang of Pakistani paedophiles has her in their direct line of sight for grooming.
>
> 'These men have decided that because Amy is the daughter of a girl they had previously groomed, and for many years had been repeatedly gang-raped, fed alcohol and drugs, and sold (or given away) over and over and over again . . . that it is also their right to have her daughter.

'Even more shocking is that Amy has a younger sister, Ruby, who is only five-years-old old. Ruby is the mirror image of her mum, Caitlin, when she was little . . .and the paedophiles are not shy in showing their interest in her either.

'Paedophiles seemed to have an insatiable appetite for Caitlin. In fact one was so excited by her cuts that he wanted to use a razor to cut her more and have some 'bloodplay'. Eventually Caitlin's cutting became a release for her, a comfort and punishment all in one. She was so numb from the constant rapes, beatings and humiliation that the only time she could feel anything was when she was cutting.

'She also kept a diary, which detailed everything. When her mum found the diary, she must have been devastated to read that her fourteen-year-old daughter had been raped in their family home. Angry, she rang Gordon who laughed and told her that Caitlin had loved it and couldn't keep her hands off of him.

'Caitlin recalls how before the rape, she often used to lay with her head on her mum's lap. But, after being raped, and, having to pleasure men in unspeakable ways, she could no longer bear to be touched in an affectionate way. Her relationship with her mum soured soon after the diary was found and eventually she had to move into a hostel.

'Gordon was still controlling Caitlin for a short while after the police were called. During her time with him, she had to see many Pakistani men. One of them saw her walking home to the hostel one evening and stopped her. He took her phone and added his number to her contacts, then used her phone to ring his – giving her no chance to provide a false number. He told her he would pick her up later...she was completely submissive.

'After seeing this man, Hassan, Gordon completely disappeared. Was this the first time that Caitlin had been 'sold' by one group of paedophiles to another? She is not sure whether any money was exchanged, but she knew that she was owned by each group and was aware of being 'given' to the next

'If Caitlin thought things were bad with Gordon

controlling and beating her, at least with him she was only expected to see one man at a time. However, in Caitlin's words, "with the Pakistani's it was a production line, it was even more humiliating". On average, there were eight men she had to see at a time. As one man was leaving the room, another was entering. Some men entered the room more than once. She was not permitted to go to the toilet and she was not allowed to wash until they had all finished with her. Sometimes other men were in the room while she was being raped and all of this was unprotected, leading to repeated STIs.

'Caitlin talks about the various locations she was taken to by these men. On many occasions, she was forced into half-renovated houses or flats with one man leading in front of her and another close behind...no chance of escape as they walked into dark buildings with no hot water and often no toilet paper. There were nearly always more men waiting inside the building.

'She's been taken to the back of takeaway shops, taxi offices (many of these men are actually taxi drivers), barber shops, car parks, quiet country roads and once she was taken to a hotel.

'These men are Muslims, yet they not only ply their victims with alcohol, they drink it themselves. With years of shocking abuse, Caitlin had trouble saying "no" to any man that propositioned her. While living at a hostel, most of the boys were also using her. She recalls a particular time one of the older boys became quite nasty because she had managed to refused his advances. He forced himself on her violently, all while the other boys were watching and laughing. After the attack was over, the watchers left and the boy who raped her sat there crying and apologized. Caitlin then hugged him and said it was okay. She doesn't understand why she did that, but she felt bad for him.

'People need to know what has happened to her, what is happening to young girls right now, what is going to happen to the girls that are currently being groomed and to the little girls that they have in their sights to start grooming. She has shown tremendous courage in opening up and telling her story, I have such admiration for her. Many professionals have disbelieved Caitlin for years. At seventeen, she had a nervous breakdown. The psychologist who treated her reported that she couldn't decide what was fact and what was fiction; she had decided that Caitlin's story was too far-fetched to be true.

'With stories chillingly similar to Caitlin's now starting to emerge in the British media, it is blatantly obvious that she has been telling the truth for all these years, yet not one person reached out to help her when she was in extreme need. Instead, they would call her a slut and a whore. She has been told to do everyone a favour and kill herself (which she has tried several times).

'With much strength, she has managed to stay away from these men for several years now, living as normal a life as she can. She is scarred not only physically, but emotionally. As mentioned in the first few paragraphs of this letter, she has two beautiful daughters. She has never been married and says she never will be; she trusts very few men and can't stand the thought of having to sleep next to anyone other than her daughters. She lives in a quiet street with her daughters' school only two minutes' walk away. Caitlin walks her girls to and from school each day.

'In England, they don't have the public school buses that we have. They often use taxi cabs and the drivers have special cards called CRB, not unlike our 'working with children' cards. These cab drivers collect children from their houses and deliver them to school. Last December, she recognized one of these cab drivers as a leader of one of the grooming sex gangs. He also saw and recognized her. This man has seen Caitlin with her two daughters and knows where she lives. On several occasions, he has attempted to force his way into her flat. On one occasion, he caught her off guard and did manage to force his way through her front door. When she told me this, she stopped there and offered no additional information. I asked if the girls were at home? Luckily, they weren't. I then had to ask her what happened next? She feels ashamed that she was not strong enough to fight back. Once again, she was raped. She has been conditioned through constant rapes and beatings to be submissive, yet she still feels that it was her fault, she should fight back harder. These men, even years after she had disappeared, think that it is their right to force their way into her home and rape her.

'She pressed no charges because the police cannot guarantee her protection. This man has asked her to find younger girls, offering to pay her for this service. While she doesn't have the strength to be able to fight this man off for her own health and wellbeing...she has an extremely strong sense of protection not only toward her own daughters, but any other girl that is a potential victim. Needless to say, she has refused to find him any girls. He also pushed money under her front door just before Christmas along with a card saying "this is a gift for you." Both the card and money were given back to this man, but he still knows where she lives, and he knows she has two daughters.

'Two weeks ago, Caitlin called a cab to take her to the train station. She uses a taxi company that she trusts. The cab arrived at her house and she got in. As he drove off, he turned his head and said, "Caitlin – where have you been? My friends have been looking for you for a long time." Her heart sank. Then he asked her about her daughter. "How is she?" "How old is she now?" "What school does she go to?" Caitlin was horrified.

'There is no escape for Caitlin in the UK; she would constantly be looking over her shoulder. She is scared, and has lived with shocking fears for more than half of her life. In Caitlin's experience, they do not take girls that are younger than twelve. Amy will turn ten in a couple of months so she thought that she had another two years of safety, two years to save up for the airfares she would need to escape, before these paedophiles attempted to take Amy and subject her to the same atrocities that they did to her. That belief was shattered only a few days ago when she spoke to her psychologist (who specializes in women who have been victims of sex trafficking). "These men are paedophiles, they have no age barrier. Your daughters are in danger now," her psychologist warned her.

'Needless to say, she is terrified. She can't sleep, she doesn't let her girls out of her sight. She has warned them not to speak to these men, no matter what they offer. They can no longer play in the park, even with their mum watching closely. They can't visit their friends, as Caitlin cannot explain to their parents why the girls can't play at the park or in the front garden, and why they would be asked not to take their eyes off of her daughters. She can't tell anyone why she suddenly seems so over-protective of her little girls. This is a burden that she has had to carry alone. Caitlin is the only person who knows the dangers and the horrors that her little girls will be subjected to if these men take them.

'Grooming gangs break these girls emotionally and physically so that they are completely submissive. These men controlled Caitlin for so long that to this day she crumbles when approached by them. They are paedophiles, they are showing interest in her only because she has daughters. They see Amy and Ruby as their next easy targets.

'Caitlin is my cousin. I have been in Australia since I was five-years-old but we have formed a very close bond, I think because she needed to reach out to someone; she was desperate to be believed. Her parents are quite closed on the subject and she cannot speak to them about it, and she was forbidden to speak to anyone else about it for fear of what people will think. They are a wonderful support when it comes to their grandchildren, but she is unable to tell them of the extreme danger they are in now in. Caitlin is applying for a Complementary Protection Visa which is provided for people who need protection but do not fit into the category of refugee. If granted, she will be given residency and the chance for a normal upbringing for the girls.

'Caitlin is an independent woman. When she told me that the girls are in immediate danger, I told her I would find a way to raise the funds. She initially refused help, she doesn't want to "bother" me. I am asking for your help. Please, help me save them.'

***

It was so powerful – but it was also my life.

While I waited to hear the outcome, I wasn't allowed to work so I struggled getting a house and somewhere for the kids to live. ACRATH was amazing though and helped pay for our rent, but I knew this wouldn't last forever.

My night terrors stopped while I was there though, and that was a huge thing. For years, I'd sit up until the early hours until I was so exhausted I'd fall asleep. I would then need to wake early to get my daughters ready and walk them to school. This took a toll on me and so I'd resorted to taking sleeping pills but that just made the nightmares worse.

As Freya wrote:

'The English mental health care system has labelled Caitlin as having Bipolar and/or Borderline Personality Disorder. She was prescribed medication to treat the disorder, but it made her more agitated and so sleepy that she was often not able to look after her own children. Since she has been living with me she is sleeping mostly without sleeping pills, no longer experiencing night terrors and she is not taking any medication for Bipolar. She is stressed, but who can blame her; her daughters' safety and wellbeing are at risk.'

That diagnosis of bipolar actually came from one doctor some years before – I think it was easier to stick that label on me than to actually tackle what I was telling them. I don't think I have it, but very few of them actually listen to me. I don't think they should just be able to say, 'you have this' and 'take this medication', when what I really needed was for someone to understand, to listen, and to address why this still affects me.

There's no doubt that I found and still find it very hard to speak to doctors or mental health professionals about this too, particularly when I was so often assigned to Asian or Pakistani men. So, I either didn't tell them everything, which made them record that there was nothing wrong with me or that I wouldn't accept help. The situation, so many times, has been this – I got an appointment. I was terrified. I could either get a taxi there or risk it being someone who knew me or had raped me, or I could walk there, passing men like that too. That was the preparation for me going to appointments where I was expected to pour my heart out, often to a man who looks just like them. The circle was never-ending. I have had to cancel appointments, or flee back home if it got too much, so they then said that I was unreliable, or that I didn't need help as I didn't turn up.

I was the one that got labelled again. I was the one that was seen as unwilling to work towards getting better. But why could no one understand? Why could no one see that there are things that could be put in place to make this easier? Well, maybe not 'easier', it will never be 'easier', but there are certainly days when the obstacles are just too much.

* * *

> 'In the weeks prior to Caitlin, Amy and Ruby arriving in Melbourne, Caitlin's parents told me that the girls would not feel comfortable going outside and playing for long, and were too afraid to step outside without a trusted adult after dark. They were happy enough to sit and play inside as that is what they are used to. They would be too afraid of spiders to walk in the bush, would be

very shy and wouldn't swim in anything except a clean public swimming pool.

'I live on five acres, which is partly bush. The day they arrived both Amy and Ruby walked with us around our property. Ruby ran ahead of us, jumped off fallen logs and swung on branches. She felt the freedom immediately. Amy, who is less adventurous, held her mum hand. She was quite nervous.

'The following day, I woke to find both girls and my grandson all playing outside together. They would jump on the trampoline, run to the swings, then disappear behind the trees. It didn't take long for Amy to feel the freedom too. Later that day both girls swam in our pool, filled with murky bore water. Two days later they were swimming in a nearby lake without fear. Kangaroos and emus wander around freely and will enter the cottages if doors are not closed. The girls played in the bush playground every day and Caitlin watched from afar, smiling and relaxed. Sending them all back to the UK will have terrible consequences for them all. First and foremost, the girls face years of pain, suffering and humiliation that no human should ever endure. The British government has ignored this problem for so many years that these grooming gangs believe that they are above the law and can do as they will with white girls.

'Caitlin now sees that little girls as young as five and six are abducted, with Asian grooming gangs being the main suspects. Please, please protect these little girls by granting them a protection visa.'

They didn't.

We would have to go home.

So in July 2014, seven months after arriving, I came back. I knew the visa application was going nowhere. I had been told by too many people too many times that it would be political suicide for the UK government to allow another country to accept me and my girls under those terms. To do so would be accepting that they couldn't protect their own citizens from these men, that they were above the law, and the only option for someone like me was to seek protection on the other side of the world.

ACRATH suggested I get in touch with an

organisation called The Medaille Trust on my return to England. They were a charity who tried to help those who had been trafficked, and I was told that they were waiting for my call. I was feeling a little stronger after being away for seven months and, although so very disappointed, thought I had it in me to try one last fight.

I dread to think what would have happened if I hadn't made that decision, if I hadn't pulled together every last bit of hope and desperation to contact them.

It felt as if my last option had been exhausted but, when I got back from Australia, I realised I had to do something. I couldn't just ignore it and spiral down again, like all the other times. No one else was going to fix this for me. To be honest, I didn't think it could be fixed at all, but I at least had some names, some groups, that I could now contact. It felt like finally people were on my side. Maybe they wouldn't be able to do anything at all, or maybe, just maybe, they would be the ones who could help me help myself.

The Medaille Trust completed all of the necessary forms for me and put in an application to the National Crime Agency Human Trafficking Centre [UKHTC].

It seemed like a very long shot to me – no one from any official organisation had ever believed me in the past, and I didn't expect that to change now.

On the main form was a list of nineteen indicators that the Trust had to tick on my behalf. I fell into eighteen of the nineteen – all but one of the categories applied to me:

- Distrustful of authorities
- Expression of fear or anxiety
- Signs of psychological trauma (including post-traumatic stress disorder)
- The person acts as if instructed by another
- Injuries apparently a result of assault or controlling measures
- Evidence of control over movement
- Found in or connected to a type of location likely to be used for exploitation
- Restriction of movement and confinement to the workplace or to a limited area
- Passport or documents held by someone else
- Lack of access to medical care
- Limited social contact

- Limited contact with family
- Perception of being bonded by debt
- Money is deducted from salary for food or accommodation
- Threats of being handed over to authorities
- Threats against individual or their family members
- Being placed in a dependency situation
- No or limited access to bathroom or hygiene facilities

The only thing I didn't score highly on was that I knew my home address.

There were further details regarding some of the categories and seeing it in black-and-white really brought it home. *Are any of these indicators of sexual exploitation present? Movement of individuals between brothels or working in alternate locations? Individuals with very limited amounts of clothing or a large proportion of their clothing is 'sexual'? Person forced, intimidated or coerced into providing services of a sexual nature? Someone other than the potential victim receives the money from clients? Health symptoms, including sexual health issues?* Yes, yes, yes, yes, yes, yes.

I was absolutely shocked when, in September 2014, I received a bit of paper that meant more to me than you could ever imagine. It read:

> 'The UKHTC Competent Authority has decided that there are reasonable grounds to believe that [Caitlin Spencer] is a victim of human trafficking.'

That was it. Just one sentence but it said so much. They believed me. They had looked at my story, looked at the evidence, and they believed me. In less than three months, a follow-up letter arrived:

> 'The case of the above-named individual has been carefully considered by the UKHTC Competent Authority. As a result of further investigations into the case, the UKHTC Competent Authority has concluded that the above individual has been trafficked.'

The decision that I was trafficked mattered – it meant someone believed me.

The Medaille Trust had put that in my original form.

I didn't know it was trafficking – I called it *seeing people I didn't want to see*. I know I have PTSD because of it all now too – I do believe the doctors who told me that, but I don't know what to do with it. It was all coming to an end. And I felt stronger than ever before.

***

I am well aware that my story is difficult on so many levels – not just because of the abuse, but because of the perpetrators. I know that I will be accused of flaming racial divisions, of giving ammunition to those who are looking for reasons to hate others because of their seeming differences. But the fact is, this is my story and this is the truth. I have a mixed-race daughter, I am not a racist person – however, I know I'll be called racist simply because I am raising a hugely uncomfortable truth. The men who abused me did so because I was white. They called me 'kafir' girl from the start. I was always a white bitch and a white slut and a white whore to them. They rarely managed to insult me without making reference to my colour, and it is my belief that the fact I was white was vitally important to them. That anyone might suggest I should keep quiet about this is part of the problem – for too long, our fear of cultural divisions has silenced women and girls. Prejudice works both ways, and I am a victim of it.

My life has been destroyed by these men. I couldn't even begin to work out how many men have sexually abused me, because I haven't even allowed myself to be present when it has happened. What do you think has to happen to someone, has to be done to them, to make them dissociate so completely?

I'm not telling my story because I hate Asian men, I'm telling it because I hope that one girl – *one* girl – reads it and knows that it wasn't her fault.

I know that there is a sense that drawing attention to this issue would make matters worse, it would inflame relations between different groups in our society, but why should it be the most vulnerable who are forced into silence? I have Muslim friends – all women – and I know there are good, kind people in that community, but I also think we are lying to ourselves if we deny that there is a problem. We can't allow our fears to let this continue. If someone is a racist, they are a racist. I'm not lying to myself and saying my story won't appeal to them – but I do hope that it will also speak to people who have simply closed their eyes to the truth for too long. Who actually do more harm than good with political naiveté. I am well aware that there are plenty of white British men who prop up the sex industry and who abuse girls too, and I suffered at their hands too, but I think that we are willing to look at that issue a lot more than we are with other groups.

Personally, I do believe that the views some Asian men have of women – whether from their social or cultural or religious beliefs – should be tackled with equality, the equality with which we should tackle all crime. These men should not be given preferential treatment because of their beliefs. They should be judged by the rules of decent society – and surely no decent society can continue to turn a blind eye to this?

Am I to remain silent when they say that I am not worthy of respect or decent treatment? Should I just keep quiet while they abuse and vilify me? When they say I am promiscuous just because I am white, that I am a whore just because I am Western? It is such a twisted logic that can say a young white girl is to be labelled as 'wild' or needs to get abuse out of her 'system', while also seeing these men as intrinsically good people just because we are too scared to look at what they really are.

It is disgusting and it is twisted – but I won't stand for it any longer . . . and, thankfully, I finally found someone else who felt exactly the same way.

CHAPTER 17

finding my voice

Baroness Cox of Queensbury, to give her the full title she carries so brilliantly, had quite the reputation on this subject. She was a well-known human rights campaigner and has been a Tory peer since the 1980s, but had such a respected background and pedigree on important issues that she was much-loved across the political spectrum. Perhaps not by everyone, but certainly by people who are willing to stick their heads above the parapet. She wasn't a women to be concerned about what was deemed politically appropriate – she just fought wherever she saw a battle that needed her. At one point, she called herself *the voice of the voiceless* and I needed her now.

She had sprung to the defence of British Muslim women, when she was horrified by the decision of the Law Society to publish 'good practice' notes for solicitors on making wills compliant with sharia, to deny women equal shares of inheritance, and exclude children born out of wedlock. 'The suffragettes will be turning in their graves,' she said. 'It undermines the most fundamental principles of equality enshrined in British law.'

Others disagreed. A fellow Lord had said: 'There is no reason why the principles of sharia law… should not be the basis for mediation or other forms of alternative dispute resolution.'

I loved Caroline's response.

'Give me a break,' she said.

This was a woman who spoke her mind. She said that sharia was seeping into enforcing divorce settlements, ignoring domestic violence and deciding access to children, all properly the preserve of British law, not something that should be tampered with.

After I was put in touch with her through The Medaille Trust, I read so many things she had been quoted on, and soon believed that this was someone who I would love to have on my side.

'In these sharia councils, men can very easily divorce women, but for Muslim women it is much harder. I had a fifty-year-old widow come to me for help because she wanted to remarry. She was told she had to have the permission of her closest living male relative, who turned out to be an eleven-year-old son, living in Jordan. She showed me where he had signed his name in childish Arabic handwriting to give permission,' she told one journalist.

'One Muslim lady who came to meet me here suffered horrific physical abuse in her marriage, ending up in hospital, yet she was under huge pressure from her community not to involve the police because it would shame her family. So, she went to a sharia court instead, which denied her a divorce and told her to go back to her abusive husband and give him another chance. He carried on abusing her. She wept as she told me about it, and I wept with her.'

Caroline had been called a racist and an Islamophobe. She had replied: 'I believe in freedom of speech. It's rubbish, of course. I'm passionate about Muslim women and yet I am called Islamophobic.'

She recognised that politicians don't, generally, want

to upset community leaders, yet 'this concern with cultural sensitivity seems to be justifying practices that contravene the fundamental qualities of our democracy – one law for everyone. If we don't act, we are condoning discrimination.' I knew all about that. I knew all about what happens when one side can throw out all of the insults and threats - and what happens to the women on the other side of it.

And then, after meeting with her for the first time in early 2015 and finally finding the courage to tell her my story, she invited me to come to the House of Lords to speak about my life so it could all finally be put on record.

***

I couldn't believe I was standing there.

Me. Caitlin Spencer. Asked to speak in the House of Lords to all of these important people. Although I was terrified, I did it. I *had* to – not just for me, but for all the other girls out there, the ones who no one was listening to.

So I told them my story:

'I'm very nervous about speaking in front of you all because I've never done anything like this before. I've written my story down because I thought it would be easier than just standing up and talking to you. So here goes, this is my story. I was the victim of Muslim grooming gangs for well over a decade. I was very young when it started.'

I told them how it all began, with Gordon coming to my house, and how abuse became my life for over a decade. I also tried to tell them that even though I was now 'safe', the mental and physical scars would stay with me forever:

'The last time I tried to commit suicide was about three weeks ago. I felt really depressed because I learned that my counselling sessions would no longer be paid for and also that two of my rapists who I thought were dead were actually alive. One of them works for the Pakistani government and one of them is a politician here. All this just pushed me over the edge.

The English "justice" system is crap. When I was around fifteen, my mum called the police. The officer sent to deal with me was intimidating. He seemed angry with me, asking me very intimate and upsetting questions. When I asked him to stop, he said I had to get used to it, as this is what I would have to deal with in court. He told me that if I were to testify, I would get no protection. For that reason, I never took it further. The police told my mother that I was a known prostitute and to leave me to it, that I'd stop when I was ready. In anger, my mum took my phone and rang Gordon. He laughed and told her what he did to me in her bed and that I loved it and couldn't keep my hands off him. After a while, I would have been just about sixteen, my mum had to kick me out because it was all getting too much. My mental state was bad, men were showing up at our home, hanging around in gangs outside the house in cars. It was too much for her and she had to protect my brother too, so I had to go. I went to live in a youth hostel, where things went from bad to worse. I was eventually controlled by a Muslim man in his forties or fifties. His name was Hassan. I have records dating back about fourteen years of me trying to get help, telling medical professionals that I was gang-raped, and them not believing me.

I have been pregnant eleven times that I know of and

have had seven abortions. My two daughters are both a result of being raped. I told the doctors about being gang-raped but they didn't believe me. Only two people ever believed me. One was a social worker and one was an occupational therapist.

In 2013 a man who had been pestering me for a long time came to my house and pushed himself through my front door. He said he wanted me to find other young girls for him. I said I didn't know any and managed to get rid of him. A couple of weeks later he put money through my door with a note saying it was a gift. He had given me his phone number so I called him and told him I didn't want his money. I arranged to meet him to return it. He still wouldn't leave me alone and even started asking how old my daughter was and what school she goes to. This is one of the reasons I went to live in Australia with relations. I've been to Australia several times to get away from them, but my children really miss their grandparents. Some still see me today and talk brazenly about the things they did, and still do to other girls. I am utterly disgusted at the lack of interest from the police and the lack of protection they have given me despite the information I have given them. I managed to track down the identity of about eighty of these men by finding one of them on Facebook and looking through his friends list. I went to tell the police. I had a meeting with two police officers but while I was giving them the names the officers stopped me because they said they had to be somewhere else. They can't have done anything about it because I still see at least five of these men in my home town driving the taxis.

The police said that for me to press charges they would have to use my name in their reports. But these rapists know where I live. They have threatened to harm my family if I go to the police. I have two young daughters. I never get into a taxi where I live because they're all run by Pakistani Muslims. But a few weeks ago, I had to use one to pick up my daughter from school because I was running late. The driver was one of my rapists. He recognised me. He said he'd recognise that face anywhere. He said I didn't give any trouble like the other girls and tried to make me see him again. He told me they have other girls now. This is the worst thing. They are still committing these crimes with other young British girls. He gave me his card. I took it so that I'd have his name and phone number. I went to the police with his details.

They wrote his details down but he's still driving around in a taxi. He's still raping other young girls.

They ruined a big part of my life. I have moved several times but it's ineffective. A bit of me feels frightened that, if they catch me on my own, I might react in the way I used to when I was younger. I'd just do what they want because it's easier than fighting them because if I did, they'd get really nasty.

But now, I am mainly angry. I can't let them win. I'm afraid, yes, but I am now doing what I can to get the message out there of what goes on with these gangs. These men find it OK to rape non-Muslim girls. It's in their culture. It's a brutal cult and needs to be stopped. They used to call me a white bitch and a whore and said 'this is what white girls are for.' It took me a long time to understand their claims about the link between Islam's teachings and what they were doing. What I want you all to do now is stop being politically correct and to deal with the truth. Admit that this is being done mainly by Pakistani Muslims, stop saying Asians. And admit that this hasn't stopped. There are other young British girls who are still suffering today in the way I suffered at the hands of men who should be behind bars. Thank you for listening.'

I was exhausted writing it all down – to see all of my life there was a shattering experience, but it gave me strength. It showed that I was a survivor, and I did feel stronger now, I truly did. With Caroline by my side, I felt as if I couldn't be ignored. She was a powerful woman, she was the right class – she was the right type in a way I had never been.

The response was more than I could have hoped for. There was silence when I spoke, and I could see Caroline out of the corner of my eye. I tried to block out other things that were sneaking in – laughter, smells, Hassan's jewelled slippers. I needed to do this even if my voice was breaking and my hands were shaking. They were all so supportive – they thanked me for being so brave and open, and said my words would be included in the evidence that would be produced.

When I left, I was a bit shell-shocked – and that's no surprise really. I have so many horrific stories to tell of my life as a sex slave to Pakistani men. Many of them are so graphic that I've wondered whether I should even put them in the minds of other people – but my story does need to be told. People have to know what has happened to me, what is happening to young girls right now, what is going to happen to the young girls that are currently being groomed, and to the girls they have in their sights to start grooming.

Many professionals have disbelieved me. And if no one believes you, there's no help and no protection; but if you tell it all, it becomes too big, it becomes too overwhelming for other people, and they would rather turn a blind eye or box it up as something else.

But I'm not the only one. There are far too many stories like mine starting to emerge, and there are finally convictions. Too few, but they are there.. They don't want to listen to girls and women who have years of abuse to disclose – they like a judge and twelve jurors to listen for them. What happens though to those of us who are told that a case can't go forward? That because, ironically, there were too many abusers and rapists to make the allegations 'stick'? I'd hope it was blatantly obvious that I've been telling the truth for all these years.

And now I finally had people on my side.

***

Through moving home so often, I've managed to stay away from the gangs for several years now. I have disappeared to these men, living as normal a life as I can. I'm still scarred, not only physically, but emotionally. These days I live in a quiet area with my children, where they go to a school directly opposite my home. I walk them to school and pick them up every single day.

Why don't I move to a different city or town? Honestly, I think they're everywhere. I do visit various cities in the UK to attend concerts sometimes. On many occasions I've either seen or been recognised by some of the Pakistani men that I used to know. They took me to a lot of different cities and I've been shared around hundreds (possibly thousands) of men.

However much support I get, however much people finally believe me, there's no escape for me in the UK. I'm constantly looking over my shoulder wherever I go. My parents are my only source of support in England – maybe that's not much, but it's all I have. I feel that I am much safer close to my family rather than move to another city, where it's possible I could be recognised by one of these men and have absolutely no one around that I could go to if anything happened.

I've been to the police, I've given names and

addresses, but the only protection they can offer me is a panic button, which would be based inside my flat (not a mobile panic button). I did actually have one of these for a time but once, when a man was trying to get into my flat, it took the police thirty munutes to respond. In the past, these men have threatened to force acid down my throat if I ever went to the police, and they weren't making me feel any more protected, so I had them remove it. I'm scared, and have lived with shocking fears for half of my life, the terror of acid paralyses me at times.

Another time the police even put cameras up at the entrance to my flat and they filmed another man trying to get in, but when they reviewed the tape they said it was too blurry to identify him, so they couldn't do anything.

They just do what they want, these men, and when reported, the law seems to overlook it. Grooming gangs break these girls emotionally and physically so that they're completely submissive, or unworthy in the eyes of the law. These men controlled me for so long that to this day I crumble when approached by them. It just terrifies me that even though I've anonymously given information to the police on these men, they are still out there, going about their lives, still driving cabs, still with permission to work with children.

When will anyone do anything about it?

epilogue

This whole process of telling my story has made me see, pretty much for the first time, just how bad things were. When you're in the middle of such horrors, you do all you can just to get through each day. I know I dissociated; I know I lost time. And I know I've blocked things out. You simply can't survive if you allow yourself to feel it all, to actually acknowledge what's happening – no one could deal with that, no one.

It has also left me with so many questions.

Why didn't the police do more? I was brought up to believe they were there to help, that if you had a problem, they were the good guys and they would do something. They have done nothing for me, and I know that they've failed so many other girls and young women.

How could my parents have left me in the middle of it all? They knew. I may have denied that in the past as I tried to justify to myself why they did nothing, but now that it's all down in black and white, I can see it for myself. They knew I was involved in something that was nasty and dark and twisted. Rather than find ways to get their own child, their own daughter, out of it, they made excuses. So, Dad told me not to cause Mum any worry. Mum said that she didn't want Dad to know the truth of it all as he would go after them. But there was cause for her to worry, and maybe, just maybe, if she had worried, then she would have made me feel that I would have been supported if I tried to get out. Now that I'm a mother myself, a mother of girls, I genuinely cannot understand how she could tell herself that it was all fine, that I wasn't in any danger. I would kill for my daughters – my mother didn't even put her arms around me and say she would try.

And what if Dad had gone after them? Would that

have been so bad? What would the outcome have been? Well, he might have scared them off, which would have been the best thing. If they'd hit back, he could have got the police involved – or if they reported him, that could have blown the whole thing open too. And I'm pretty sure that the word of one man, the word of a father trying to protect his daughter, would have been given much more credence than any complaint I could have raised.

I've made so many excuses for them both for so long, but writing this has made the scales fall from my eyes. Why didn't they protect me? Why didn't they fight for me? Why didn't they think I was worth it? My mum saw me with these men. She answered the door when they rang the bell and asked for me. She saw the taxis and cars outside waiting for me so they could take me to be raped. And she let it all slide – she just accepted that policeman's word that I was a bit wild and that I would grow out of it.

How?

HOW?

How can a mother – a father – actually do that?

I've questioned whether it was my fault and until now,

I've always convinced myself that it was. I wasn't what they wanted or needed from a daughter: I let them down. I was an embarrassment, a disgrace. But I can see it now: I was a child. A child who should have been protected by someone, a child who had nowhere to turn and whose lack of support made her a perfect victim. I wasn't really that different from those girls from the residential homes, or the ones who were street prostitutes when they were barely in their teens. All of us were lost, and all of us ended up trapped. Maybe we weren't all kept under lock and key, but the mental and emotional prisons which held us were just as secure, just as unlikely to be left behind.

acknowledgements

One of the nicest parts of this journey – and, at the start, I didn't think there would be any nice parts at all! – has been finding out that there are good people out there. Anyone who believed me seemed like a miracle. That I ended up with a group of people around me while I told my story has been a source of tremendous support and encouragement. When this all began, I never thought there would be so many to thank, but there are, and that is a miracle in itself.

My ghostwriter, Linda Watson-Brown, for making all of this possible. I could never have done it without you. I'm so lucky to have had you by my side through the process. Thank you for being so patient and understanding, for never giving up on me and for fighting to help me tell my story. I couldn't have hoped for anyone better.

When Linda told me she hoped we'd work with her favourite editor, I trusted her – when that happened and I met Ciara Lloyd, I realised there was someone else on my side, and that the journey would hopefully be a little easier for having her there. To her and the team at John Blake Publishing, my sincere thanks.

To Baroness Caroline Cox – you and Sam have been so supportive and helpful through so many things, and I would always want you on my team. You have helped my voice get heard in so many ways. I'm blessed to have you as a friend.

To Fiona Bruce for listening to my story and also for being a great support. You are truly a lovely lady and I appreciate all you have done – I hope we can work together in the future to throw light on these awful things.

The Medaille Trust has recognised me as a trafficked person from the start and supported me through the

National Crime Agency process so that they could look at my situation and come to the same conclusion. That piece of paper means a great deal to me. I'd also like to thank them for helping to cover much-needed therapy for an extended time.

Of course, I want to thank my kids, my beautiful girls. They're my reason to breathe, to move on to a much happier and better life. I never want them to read my book, but I still want to say that I love them so much and I'm so proud of them. Without knowing it, they gave me the strength to do this, and I will always fight for them.

My cuddly, loving dogs need to be thanked too! For being a great source of support and safety, for never judging me and for giving me a reason to get out of bed some days. When I wake up to them snoring away in my bed after one of my nights of terror, I'm grounded in desperately-needed reality by them so quickly.

The close friends and family who know all of me and my past and have decided to stay anyway. The ones who have supported, encouraged and pushed me in the right direction and kept me on the right path. My cousin and her family for getting me and the kids out of a bad situation and giving us a safe place to stay, for making sure we had everything we needed while we were there, and for being so understanding. Kathy, who works for an anti-trafficking NGO in Australia, also needs a special mention for helping to make our lives so much easier (and fun) while we were there as she helped to get the kids into school and arranged everything we needed. I'm so glad to still be in contact with you and to call you a friend.

Finally, to everyone who has taken the time to read this. I know it's difficult, I know no one wants to think these things are happening – but just by being willing to take the first step and pick up this book, you have shown that you're different, that you might be able to do something. Please, please, if this has touched you in any way, look after your daughters. Keep them close. Watch where they go, listen to them, believe them. Open your eyes to what's going on in your towns and cities, never think it can't happen to someone you know or in the area you live. It is everywhere.

I can't use my real name for this book because I'm still in danger. I desperately hope that by speaking out, other girls and women will know they are not alone. If you do need help, please contact a support group and please don't think you can't escape this.

There is hope for you.

There is hope for me.

Thank you for listening.

Caitlin x

my girls...

My girls...

I know that I need to think I matter, but I have a problem with that. There are two people who matter so much more – and I have no problem at all in telling them how much they are loved.

My darling girls, my fatherless girls – you are of me, I made you and I adore you. I will always do all I can to protect you and I will always be so grateful that you are in my life. I would say that I'd lay down my life for you but I need to keep fighting – I know now that I'm no use to you if I'm not here.

I'm not sure if you'll ever read this but I need to write these words. Who knows what will become of me, but I want the pair of you to change the world. I want you to be strong and independent, to know that you are your own women, and to never, ever do anything just because you feel you are too broken to be entitled to choices.

Amy – my beautiful Amy. We have our battles, don't we? What can I say about you? You make my world and you try to destroy it at times too! You adore animals and I adore you for that. You have a kindness and gentleness with other creatures that I hope you carry in you forever, and I really hope that came from me. I see you melt with our fur babies, and I see the little girl in you at those moments.

You are such a sensible, polite, thoughtful girl who cares so deeply for those around you. Even if you fall out with someone, you'll be there for them in a flash if they need you again. You are strong-willed and you are stubborn, and you always voice your opinion if you disagree with things and I do try to leave you to do that because it will serve you well. Always stand up for yourself, and for others if you can, because the world needs girls like you and it needs the woman you will become.

I need to be a boring Mum now though Amy – stop wearing so much make-up! You don't need it and you take about three hours to get ready when we go out. I don't think we're doing too badly if that's the only problem though, do you? And, actually, you can fight me on it if you want because I love that you aren't submissive, I love that you know your own mind. I love that you are you.

Ruby – my darling Ruby.

You have such a way with animals too and I think that is where your life will lead you (can I come too?). You have such a way with them, with your gentleness and thoughtfulness. You put everyone else first – always with a smile on your face, always with that essence of sweetness that has been there since you were that tiny little baby I adored from the first second.

I hope your shyness protects you, I hope it keeps you away from anyone who might wish to do you harm. I also hope that your naturally inquisitive nature will make you see the world as a wonderful place, that you will have that pleasure in life that I never had, that will take you to fantastic places and opportunities.

You are so clever (thank God for Google as I can't

keep up with your questions!), always wanting to do maths, always doing so well in school. I smile when I see you do your acrobatics around the house, I smile when I see you so happy in just being you, and I do feel a little bit of pride that you have the freedom to be that way.

I want you both to be protected forever and I want you to know I love you fiercely. It doesn't matter where you came from – you are 100% mine, I only think of you as mine, no one else is involved. I want you to be happy and safe – that's all, not much to ask.

Stay with me forever, girls. Indulge me when I say I want to run away with you both and live amongst the penguins. I love you so very much and I wouldn't change you for the world. You are my reason to be here. You are the light I thought I would never see. You are all that matters.

You are the best last chapter in the world.

I love you

Mum xx